To Carol,

May all your efforts in love

Happy ending.

Tom Myu

W9-CFK-773

GOLDILOCKS
on
MANAGEMENT

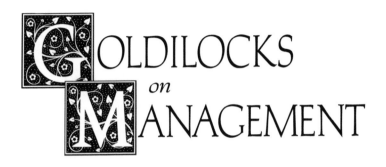

GOLDILOCKS on MANAGEMENT

27 Revisionist Fairy Tales for Serious Managers

Gloria Gilbert Mayer & Thomas Mayer

Illustrations by Michael Zaharuk

AMACOM
American Management Association

New York • Atlanta • Boston • Chicago • Kansas City • San Francisco • Washington, D.C.
Brussels • Mexico City • Tokyo • Toronto

Special discounts on bulk quantities of AMACOM books are available to corporations, professional associations, and other organizations. For details, contact Special Sales Department, AMACOM, an imprint of AMA Publications, a division of American Management Association.
1601 Broadway, New York, NY 10019.
Tel.: 212-903-8316   Fax: 212-903-8083

This publication is designed to provide accurate and authoritative information in regard to the subject matter covered. It is sold with the understanding that the publisher is not engaged in rendering legal, accounting, or other professional service. If legal advice or other expert assistance is required, the services of a competent professional person should be sought.

Library of Congress Cataloging-in-Publication Data

Mayer, Gloria G.
Goldilocks on management : 27 revisionist fairy tales for serious
    managers / Gloria Gilbert Mayer and Thomas Mayer.
        p.   cm.
    Includes index
    ISBN 0-8144-0481-2
    1. Management.   2. Fairy Tales.   I. Mayer, Thomas R.   II. Title.
HD31.M347 1999
658—dc21   99-31250
                                                                  CIP

© 1999 Gloria Gilbert Mayer and Thomas Mayer.
All rights reserved.
Printed in the United States of America.

This publication may not be reproduced,
stored in a retrieval system,
or transmitted in whole or in part,
in any form or by any means, electronic,
mechanical, photocopying, recording, or otherwise,
without the prior written permission of AMACOM,
an imprint of AMA Publications, a division of
American Management Association,
1601 Broadway, New York, NY 10019.

Printing number

10 9 8 7 6 5 4 3 2 1

CONTENTS

"If you really read the fairy tales, you will observe that one idea runs from one end of them to the other—the idea that peace and happiness can only exist on some condition. This idea, which is the core of ethics, is the core of the nursery tale."

G. K. Chesterton, *All Things Considered*

Fairy tales offer us fundamental truths that have persisted across generations. They are simple, direct, fun, and enduring.

Fairy tales define the underlying beliefs of any society as accurately as its wisest philosophers do. (In Norway, Hans Christian Andersen is considered a philosopher and social reformer.) Consequently, fairy tales have an underlying significance that reflects a deeply held value system. Each fairy tale is an ecumenical parable designed to develop the listener's moral and ethical values.

In our three decades of involvement in management, we have seen a variety of trends come and go. Virtually all of them have created little enduring impact. Yet when we evaluated what we have accomplished as consultants and managers over the years, we discovered that the actual issues involved are often quite simple and basic.

We have learned that when we tap in to people's basic moral and ethical beliefs, we accomplish much more than when we facilitate some carefully crafted, well-timed, and professionally correct encounter. In short, we discovered that most of us were actually best prepared for our future success before we even got on our first school bus.

This book recaptures our youth, taking the classic fairy tales we loved back then and revealing the underlying business management lesson inherent in each tale. We have, however, updated each such story a bit, using elements of contemporary business culture to make each tale more adult, more reflective of our professional lives, and more fun.

Though its approach is playful, *Goldilocks on Management* is not intended as a parody of management books. We have some very real (and quite important) observations to make here, so please take us just as seriously as you took fairy tales when you were a child.

We should perhaps add that none of the principles we present in this book are new. But by illustrating these principles with twenty-seven of the classic stories we all know and love (as well as with contemporary case histories), we hope that you will appreciate those enduring principles in a new and deeper way.

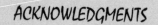

ACKNOWLEDGMENTS

To Moe, Rose, Howard, and Elaine, our parents, to whom we owe our first exposure to the wonderful world of fairy tales. And also to Kimberly and Jeffrey, our children, who gave us the opportunity to pass on the tradition.

1. GOLDILOCKS AND THE THREE BEARS

Executive Summary

family of bears owns and operates The Bruin House, a budget motel deep in the forest. It is clean and well maintained, and the Bear family has made a nice living from it for several years. The motel's ads proudly proclaim, "We've got a comfortable bed that's just your size." Indeed, to better serve its diverse customer base, the motel has outfitted its rooms with beds of various lengths.

One Monday in the middle of the slow season, the three bears sit down to a late-night snack of porridge and milk. "Ow!" says Mama Bear after taking her first spoonful. "I left it in the microwave too long again."

"Hey, Mom," says Baby Bear. "Just what is porridge, anyway? All the other cubs say I'm a wimp for eating it."

Papa Bear stands up. "All right, enough whining," he says. "Let's all go take a walk until our porridge cools down." And the family goes outside for a brief stroll.

A few minutes later, a woman drives up and parks in the lot. She is the head of sales and marketing for an institutional food products firm, and she has just had a very bad day. In the past eight hours, she has lost the accounts of two major hotel chains, locked her keys in the car, lost her way on the rural highways, and arrived at three roadside restaurants just after they have stopped serving. During the past hour she has gotten a flat tire, which she had to change herself—not an easy task for a woman only five feet tall. To top it off, she has just driven past a half dozen motels, all with NO VACANCY signs.

Exhausted, hungry, and irritable, she enters the lobby and looks around. "Hello!" she shouts. No one answers.

She looks into the dining room, which is closed. "Of course," she mutters to herself. "The worst day of Goldilocks Czarniecki's life has to be awful right up until the stroke of midnight."

She walks to the darkened hostess station, picks up a menu, and looks it over. It offers mostly standard motel fare, though an unusually large number of dishes feature berries. She is puzzled also by the note at the bottom that boasts, "All entrées served with all the honey you can eat." The prices are on the high side, which makes her wonder if the motel's owners are paying too much for their food products. She begins giving herself a mental pep talk. *All right, Goldy girl, you've still got a chance to turn this day around a little bit. Maybe you can at least add The Bruin House to your stable of smaller accounts.*

She returns to the deserted lobby and looks impatiently at the door to the Bear family's apartment. It is slightly ajar, so she pushes it open and walks inside. "Is anyone home?" she shouts, but she is greeted only by silence once again.

She wanders into the dining room and spies the three steaming bowls of porridge on the table. Suddenly she is ravenous with hunger, and she cannot resist picking up a spoon and taking a bite from the biggest bowl. The hot porridge immediately burns the inside of her mouth, and she leaps back, rubbing her cheek to ease the pain. *Great*, she thinks, *now I'm injured, too.* But as soon as the pain begins to subside, she thinks, *I wonder* *what they're paying for this. I'll bet it's more than the $17.80 we charge for a fifty-pound bag.*

Still terribly hungry, she takes a spoonful of porridge from another bowl, but finds it cold and unappetizing. Dispiritedly, she tries the porridge in the smallest bowl. To her surprise, it is just the right temperature and consistency. Eagerly, she sits down in the tiny chair in front of the bowl and begins eating. But a moment later the chair collapses under her weight, and she falls to the floor amid pieces of wood and strips of rattan.

Perfect, Goldilocks thinks. *I've managed to break into someone's home, eat their food, and destroy their property. This morning I was a highly compensated professional woman with a thriving career. Tonight I've become a common criminal with a serious attitude problem.* Sobbing, she staggers into the adjacent bedroom and collapses on the biggest of three beds. *I just want to curl up and sleep for the rest of the winter,* she tells herself sadly.

Almost immediately her back begins to hurt because the bed is extremely hard. She sighs, gets up, and falls on the slightly smaller bed beside it. Instantly she can tell that the bed is far too soft, so she rises again and drops into the smallest bed. To her relief, it is extremely comfortable, cozy, and welcoming. She pulls the covers over her head, wipes the remaining tears from her eyes, and quickly falls into a deep, dream-filled sleep.

In her dream, her personal coach appears. "Goldilocks," she says, "this may not be your finest hour, but it's an opportunity nevertheless. You're an award-winning saleswoman. You've increased your company's customer base by 19 percent in only three years. You've got good products and the will to succeed. Don't just lie there bemoaning your fate—get up and turn this encounter into a sale!"

While Goldilocks is receiving this unconscious pep talk, the Bear family returns home. "What's this?" Papa Bear growls, looking at the smashed chair and the overturned bowl of porridge. "Some gang has broken in. As if we don't have enough problems already."

He looks into the bedroom. "Oh, my goodness. Someone's sleeping in our son's bed." He rushes into the bedroom and says loudly, "So, lady, maybe you want to explain what you're doing, snoring away in our bedroom?"

Startled, Goldilocks leaps out of bed, lost in a fog of sleep and inspirational messages. "Good evening!" she says enthusiastically. "Let's talk about porridge prices. And service, too. No one can beat us when it comes to service."

Papa Bear stares at her, then looks at his wife. "She's crazy. Don't come in."

"Sir," Goldilocks says brightly, "we're known throughout the industry for competitive prices and superior services. Let me give you an example of how we go the extra mile for our customers."

"Call the police," Papa Bear says over his shoulder to his wife.

"Don't do that," Goldilocks says half-pleadingly. "Look, if you don't bring the police into it, I'll give you a special price on berries. I can probably cut you a deal on honey, too."

Papa Bear growls loudly. "You idiot! You break into our home, destroy our furniture, and frighten our son, and you want to talk honey prices? People have been mauled for less."

Terrified, Goldilocks screams and runs. As the Bear family watches, she flees the apartment, stumbles through the lobby, and leaps into her car. She guns the engine and drives away into the darkness at top speed.

"So, little one," Papa Bear says to Baby Bear as the taillights recede into the distance. "You wanted to know what porridge is. I'll tell you what it is: a pain in the butt."

Basic Lesson

> **Sales and negotiation strategies must be carefully planned and implemented to be effective.**

Applications for Serious Managers

In her brief but disastrous dealings with the Bear family, Goldilocks failed as both a salesperson and a negotiator. Instead of acting strategically and working from a solid knowledge base, she relied on little more than enthusiasm and energy. Worse, she acted impulsively, basing her decisions on emotions rather than sound, reasoned judgment. Lastly, in a high-stakes situation she compromised too much (and too quickly), immediately losing what little credibility and negotiating position she may have had. It is no wonder that the story ends with Goldilocks fleeing, her tail between her legs.

In business, the stakes in negotiation can be high, and serious negative consequences can result if too much is compromised or negotiations break down. Therefore, it is essential not only to learn and practice negotiating techniques but also to plan a negotiation strategy.

In any good-faith negotiation, the aim is to create a win-win situation. Yet when conflicts arise, resolution can only occur when three things take place: (1) the problem is identified correctly; (2) both parties focus on the end solution; and (3) personal agendas are separated from the problem.

There is also the thorny issue of how much compromise is appropriate. Too little can create the classic lose-lose situation in which both parties dig in their heels and wait for the other to back down. Too much can create a win-lose situation in which only one party comes away from the table with what it wants or needs.

To begin with, you must understand your own position fully. This includes each aspect of its goals, needs, and fallback positions, as well as its bottom line for the negotiation process. What is most important? What can you legitimately give up? What happens if you walk away? How much leverage do you truly have? What is the timeline for making a final decision? What do you know about the other side and its negotiating team? Before an appropriate negotiation strategy can be planned and implemented, these questions need to be answered in a closed-door session, with the head negotiators having a clear understanding of their company's position on all of these issues. The negotiation teams should not meet until all of these questions have been answered.

The seven basic steps in any negotiation process are:

1. Getting acquainted with one another and the organizations you each represent
2. Defining the goals and objectives of the negotiating session
3. Promptly completing any discussions on simple and/or uncontested matters

4. Discussing disagreements and areas of conflict
5. Looking for alternative solutions that may serve both parties or address both their concerns
6. Compromising and reevaluating positions
7. Reaching a suitable agreement

Because people can easily misinterpret points or "forget" compromises they have agreed to, it is critical that someone be assigned to take the minutes of each negotiation session. These minutes should be read aloud at the end of the session, and both parties should approve them (or raise any objections immediately) before they leave. This practice not only removes any uncertainty or confusion, but it ensures that everyone is clear about what decisions, action items, and concessions have been agreed to.

In a negotiating session, everyone has something to give and something to gain. One of the biggest mistakes is thinking that you can (or should) win too big, especially if a contract covers only a year or two. Even though the people you are negotiating with on the other side may definitely need your business right now, if they have to give up too much to get your contract, they may begin planning a way to walk away next time there's something to negotiate. (Or they may simply plan to take their business elsewhere in the future.)

It should go without saying that it is counterproductive to get angry at the other side's negotiating team. If the negotiations run into problems, it is rarely the fault of the people doing the bargaining; more likely, the cause is the organization or the negotiating process itself—perhaps both.

Ideally, a successful negotiation ends with the teams on both sides having lunch or dinner together. And if your side has won a major concession, we suggest you pick up the tab as a goodwill gesture.

A Real-World Business "Tale"

Robert Mbuto was an optometrist who owned his own eyeglass and contact lens shop in a Boston suburb. His shop was extremely busy, and over the years he had hired three junior partners. Although Robert owned 51 percent of the business, he relied on his partners for advice and guidance and treated them as equals.

After fifteen years in business, Robert received an offer from a national chain of optical centers to buy his operation. The sale would make Robert a multimillionaire and allow him to retire at any time. Nevertheless, he felt committed to his partners and wanted their input before making a final decision.

Robert described the offer to his partners during their next monthly staff meeting. He explained that he liked the idea of selling the business, but wanted to negotiate the best deal he could—a deal that would allow his partners to achieve their own goals for the future. His partners, though at first shocked that Robert would want to sell the store, agreed to work with him to negotiate the best deal he could for all of them.

Robert scheduled two planning meetings with his partners before meeting with representatives from the national firm. For the first planning session, Robert hired a consultant to assist the four of them in articulating their goals. Although at first everyone assumed that the primary goals were financial, after much discussion all four partners agreed that their goals involved professional fulfillment and autonomy, time for further professional education, and time for their families, vacations, and other nonprofessional fulfillment.

The second planning meeting was devoted to negotiating points and strategies. The partners identified what was most important to them and what positions would be deal breakers. They also discussed other options. For example, if the deal didn't happen, would they offer the store to other national chains?

Robert knew another optometrist who had sold his own business to the same national firm two years earlier. Robert called his colleague and got as much information as he could about the company, its methods of operation, and its negotiating team.

Because of all of this careful focusing, information gathering, and planning, Robert went into the first negotiating session feeling that he was well prepared. He had a good understanding of what he and his partners wanted, what they were willing to compromise on, and when he would have to say no and walk out.

The four things that Robert insisted on were: (1) the purchase price; (2) a long-term employment agreement for all four partners; (3) substantial time off for professional education and vacations; and (4) the partners' approval of any new operating policy and procedure, with such approval to be withheld only when the change would interfere with the quality of care.

The negotiations proceeded relatively smoothly. Both sides reached an agreement on price fairly quickly. The national chain was willing to agree to a long-term employment arrangement for the four partners, although Robert had to compromise somewhat on the salary each optometrist wanted and on the hours of operation (all of the chain's shops had to be open seven days a week).

Two sticky points remained, however: time off and the partners' right to approve new procedures and policies. Negotiators from the national chain insisted that all four partners be in the store a minimum of forty-eight weeks a year. Robert held firm on this issue, however. "For each of the past nine years," he said, "each of us has taken seven weeks off for vacation and professional education. That free time is one of the major reasons we're working together. None of us wants to give that up—and frankly, since we're running a highly successful business, none of us has any reason to."

Robert also refused to back down on the partners' right to review any proposed changes in policy or procedure. "We only want veto power on those changes that could affect the quality of care," he said. "If your company won't allow us to ensure that our patients get the best care, then we don't want to sell you our business. It's that simple."

In the end, the national chain gave in on both issues, and most of the other salient points were agreed upon before the attorneys got involved. Although the lawyers delayed the sale for five months, negotiating every word, eventually Robert and his partners sold the business and everyone was fairly happy with the final terms.

The Bottom Line

While some people are by nature better negotiators than others, effective selling and negotiating skills require more than just talking well, listening carefully, and knowing how and when to compromise. The real work of negotiation takes place before the two sides even begin talking. Unless your own position has first been carefully clarified and refined, you simply cannot negotiate or sell effectively, because you aren't yet certain about what is

important, what is not, and what is so crucial that it can't be bar-
gained away at any price.

Our poor impulsive Goldilocks could learn this important
lesson from Robert Mbuto: Success comes far more readily (and
far more frequently) when you think, evaluate, and plan before
you act.

2. JACK AND THE BEANSTALK

Executive Summary

ack is a disadvantaged child living in poverty with his single mother. They rent a tumbledown, substandard dwelling that is not up to code; an old cow is their sole possession. They decide to liquidate this asset to fend off starvation, so Jack is sent to negotiate the best deal in the marketplace.

In a nontraditional transaction, Jack acquires a handful of magic beans in exchange for the cow. Although this asset swap avoids state and federal taxes, as well as any time-consuming paperwork, it does little to impress Jack's mother, who throws the beans out the window in frustration.

However, the beans fulfill their promise, and the following day a beanstalk appears that grows into the clouds. This gives Jack access to a previously untapped market monopolized by a giant.

Jack cashes in with sweat equity to gain an insider's knowledge of the local economy and consequently is able to acquire a goose that lays golden eggs. Although a dispute over property rights to the goose ensues with the giant, Jack is able to quash that challenge by axing the beanstalk as the giant tries to penetrate Jack's traditional marketplace. The downside of this settlement is that Jack loses his access to this newly established market. However, the transaction provides Jack and his mother with a substantial annuity for an extended time period.

15

Basic Lesson

> **Innovative solutions result from "outside the box" thinking.**

Applications for Serious Managers

While thinking "outside the box" is given significant lip service, few managers are truly willing to take the risks of nontraditional approaches. Like Jack's mother, they would often prefer to sell their liquid assets for hard cash. While this may directly resolve some short-term problems, it fails to develop any long-term solutions.

Such a short-term strategy is typically supported on the personal level as well: You cannot get in trouble for doing what everyone expects you to do. However, it's not likely to yield significant gains for either you or your organization.

Not every nontraditional approach will result in a goose laying golden eggs in perpetuity, of course. Nevertheless, unless some element of innovation is involved, an organization has little chance of keeping up with changing conditions and markets. If you always do what you've always done, you will always get what you've always got. Encouraging and supporting nontraditional approaches is essential to success.

Although change will always be a part of innovation, great risk does not necessarily have to be. Jack risked starvation in acquiring his magic beans; in climbing the beanstalk to a new domain, he risked being squashed out of existence by the powerful, highly competitive giant. Clearly, Jack could have lost considerably more than he gained.

Normally, the risks you and your organization take should be of a lesser magnitude. Except in extreme circumstances such as Jack's, any potential rewards should more than merit the risk taken.

Some failures will always occur, however, and these must be accepted as easily as the successes. If they are not, the unspoken message to your staff is that attempting nontraditional solutions creates a personal risk that exceeds the potential organizational rewards.

A Real-World Business "Tale"

The president of a real estate company faced a significant problem in communicating with several hundred agents in forty-plus offices scattered across seven counties. New information appeared daily that was critical to each agent's functioning—interest rates, mortgage availability, details on lenders, announcements of sales meetings, and updated advertisements. Yet many agents complained that they weren't being kept up-to-date on information as it presented itself.

The problem was compounded by the fact that many agents worked part-time and many (both part-timers and full-timers) worked primarily from their home offices. While all agents had some computer skills, only about 60 percent had both computers and modems. Everyone was on the voice-mail system, but company policy reserved its use exclusively for client access. Most had access to fax machines, but the transmission of numerous pages each day was slow and costly and tied up machines that were needed for other purposes.

The president and her immediate administrative staff considered the options of e-mail, programmable fax machines, networked voice mail, messenger services, and interoffice memo distribution. Although she was aware that her agents were frustrated by their lack of timely access to critical information, she was also concerned about the time, cost, and complexity of having to use multiple systems to provide timely information to everyone.

Then one administrative staff member made the crucial observation that management's only real responsibility was to make information available in a timely, accessible manner—not necessarily deliver it. He suggested that a dedicated, toll-free hot line be established. Any agent could call this number at any time for complete, up-to-date information.

Two weeks later, the system was up and running. Now, by 6 P.M. each business day, the administrative staff compiles that day's new information. The most critical information is placed on a dedicated voice-mail system, along with a description of what other new but less important information is available. In addition, a hard copy of more detailed information is sent to one secretary in each office via a programmable fax machine.

Now, all agents can call in for a daily update at their convenience. Each agent is responsible for making this call, deciding what information is personally significant, and then requesting more detailed information from the secretary at the appropriate office the following day.

The cost of this approach is quite small, the administrative effort involved is fairly modest, and the responsibility for who gets what information (and when they get it) has been shifted from top management to the individual agent.

Everyone in the organization is highly satisfied with this innovative solution.

The Bottom Line

Managers need to identify, encourage, and reward nontraditional actions that lead to innovative solutions. More important, they must tolerate the results of nontraditional actions and decisions, even when they do not fulfill their potential.

The "beanstalk effect" thrives only in the fertile environment of personal security arising from managerial tolerance. Anything less and the likelihood of finding magic beans in your company is about the same as finding golden eggs in your local supermarket.

3. LITTLE RED RIDING HOOD

Executive Summary

ittle Red Riding Hood is asked to courier several valuable commodities—grains, sugar, and dairy products, all processed into cakes—to her ailing grandmother, who lives on the other side of the woods.

Red Riding Hood has never been to Grandma's house alone before. She and her mother have made an oral agreement that she will not dawdle along the way. When she is halfway through the woods, however, a large wolf appears. He is wearing an Armani suit and a Rolex, and he quickly falls in step beside her. "Good afternoon," he says. "Tell me, child, what business are you on?"

Red Riding Hood says, "I'm making a delivery to my grandma on the other side of the woods. It's urgent. My mother insisted on same-day service."

"I see," says the wolf. "And did your mother request standard or preferred delivery?"

Little Red Riding Hood stops and looks at the wolf. "What do you mean?"

"Well, if all you do is schlep over to Grandma's house, hand her the package, then hurry back to your home base, that's standard service. But if you want to impress your recipient by adding value, you can stop for a few minutes, pick some flowers, and present them with your package, along with a smile and a curtsy. Of course, that's only if your family organization values superior service."

"Oh, but it does," says Red Riding Hood. "I think I'll stop right now and pick some of these beautiful wildflowers for Grandma."

"Good idea," says the wolf. He then bids her good-bye, trots on over to Grandma's house, and gobbles her up in one big, sudden gulp, like a multinational corporation acquiring a corner grocery. Then he pulls on Grandma's nightgown, puts on her glasses, and climbs into bed.

Her arms laden with flowers, Red Riding Hood soon arrives at her grandmother's house. She goes inside and hurries into the bedroom. "Hi, Grandma!" she says brightly. "I brought you cakes from my mom and flowers from the forest." She smiles and curtsies gaily.

The wolf claps. "Well done," he says. "Come closer, my dear."

Little Red Riding Hood approaches the bed. "Gosh, Grandma," she says, "why is your voice so deep and why are your eyes and ears and hands so big?"

"They're ergonomically designed for maximum efficiency and productivity," the wolf replies.

"Oh. But why are you wearing a Rolex?"

"Why, to tell the time, dear."

"Oh, of course! And what time is it now?"

"Dinner time!" With that, the wolf leaps out of the bed and devours Red Riding Hood in one gulp.

The wolf is tired after all this food and activity, so he lies back down in Grandma's bed to take a nap.

Soon he falls into a deep sleep. In fact, he begins snoring so loudly that a wildlife management consultant who is passing by hears him. Concerned, the consultant enters, goes to the bedroom, and surveys the scene. Having seen several such involuntary mergers before, he quickly identifies the problem. He kills the wolf, cuts open his stomach, and there finds both Red Riding Hood and Grandma, wet and frightened, but unharmed. He helps them out and, after collecting a substantial fee for his services from Grandma, urges Red Riding Hood to tell her mother the entire story and never talk to strangers again.

Basic Lesson

> **Competitors will take advantage of inexperience.**

Applications for Serious Managers

Little Red Riding Hood had good intentions, a clear job description, and even good instructions from her mother—but her inexperience was her downfall.

First, Red Riding Hood failed to follow established procedures in carrying out her assigned tasks and thus quite literally fell prey to the tactics and strategies of her direct competitor.

Second, Red Riding Hood gave away too much information to her chief competitor—enough to enable him to identify and locate a specific target (Grandma), then plan and implement a strategy for devouring her.

Third, her inexperience led her to trust the wolf rather than her own perception. Although Red Riding Hood recognized some anomalies in Grandma's appearance (i.e., she now had much bigger hands, ears, and eyes), she nevertheless played right into the wolf's paws.

Her biggest mistake, however, was in failing to acknowledge her own inexperience. Had she been more acutely aware of her own limitations, she would have proceeded with a great deal more caution. In particular, she would have exercised due diligence in checking out the identity of the person in the bedroom.

Had Red Riding Hood sufficiently doubted the identity of the creature in the nightgown and been more thorough in investigating the situation, she would not have asked for a mere handful of simple explanations. Instead, she might have asked for a demonstration of grandmotherly skills. For instance, she might have inquired about Grandma's knitting and asked Grandma to show her a new stitch. (A brief workshop on interviewing skills led by any competent human resources professional would probably have done Red Riding Hood a world of good.)

In short, Red Riding Hood would have brought down her entire family organization if she hadn't been saved by someone with more experience in the field.

A Real-World Business "Tale"

Roger McGuire was a new MBA who had just graduated with honors from UCLA's Andersen School of Business. His undergraduate degree was from Brown University, plus he had worked for two years at a consulting firm as an administrative assistant before attending graduate school. Roger was smart, ambitious, eager to learn, and personable. When he was with the consulting firm, he volunteered for special projects, put in extremely long hours, and was known for having tremendous potential.

A small manufacturing company that made coffee cup insulators recruited Roger. This was a start-up business, and Roger was excited by the possibility of a stock offering within the next three years. The company had an active research and development section where several new products were being researched.

Roger was hired as the assistant vice president of sales and marketing. He reported to Maria Estevez, the vice president of sales and marketing.

For the first few months, Roger did an excellent job assisting Maria and learning the business. He went on many sales calls with Maria and had good follow-through. Everyone thought he was terrific, and he was promised stock options after the initial pubic offering.

During an extremely busy time, Maria asked Roger to go on a sales call alone. The customer was a representative for a nationwide bagel chain that wanted to purchase several products for its entire chain of restaurants. However, at the upcoming sales meeting, the only thing to be specifically negotiated was coffee cup insulators.

Maria asked Roger if he needed assistance or wanted to practice first, but he felt ready and wanted to demonstrate his skill. After reviewing some written documentation about the company and a few contracts with customers, he went on the call.

Roger began the meeting by introducing himself and briefly discussing his schooling and honors. Immediately, this told the negotiators from the bagel chain that he was young and inexperienced.

The discussion then turned to his company's insulators. Roger explained why they were superior, mentioned some of his company's satisfied customers, and in general represented the product well.

Now the topic became price. Roger explained that the price was related to the size of an order. The bagel company executives stated that they had plans for major expansion across the United States and hoped to establish long-term relationships with vendors. Roger then casually mentioned the range of prices for the insulators, from the lowest to the highest, and stated again that volume determined price.

The bagel company executives insisted on the lowest price Roger had mentioned, repeating over and over that "in the future we hope to be placing orders in the millions or tens of millions of units," but formally committing to nothing. Roger, wanting to close his first solo sale, gave the negotiators the lowest price. No sliding scale was developed, no volumes were actually mentioned, and no long-term agreement was made. There was only a very low price for coffee insulators.

Roger knew something didn't go right, but was not exactly sure what it was.

Roger was lucky that he did not have signature authority for this deal. Maria, his boss, was able to salvage the situation. She told the bagel executives that the company would honor the price Roger had quoted, but insisted on a firm commitment in return. She got the bagel company negotiators to agree to a five-year contract at the rate Roger had specified.

The Bottom Line

As organizations downsize—and as it becomes more difficult to obtain experienced help in many fields—management sometimes sends out well-intentioned but inexperienced people to secure important accounts or negotiate important contracts.

This can be a major—and very costly—mistake. Note, however, that the fault lies not with the inexperienced salesperson or negotiator—who is, after all, doing his best—but with the managers who entrust talented and highly motivated people with too much too soon.

Teach such highly motivated people well, mentor them thoroughly, and in time they will be worth their weight in gold. Let them loose too soon and they could do your organization—and themselves—more harm than good.

4. THE THREE LITTLE PIGS

Executive Summary

hree small pigs each decide to seek their fortune. After updating their resumes and attending various training seminars, they withdraw their life savings from the bank and set off in search of opportunity.

The first little pig attended a training session called Living Well on Less, which was sponsored by a company that was down-sizing. He buys some straw and uses it to build a very inexpensive house. Pleased with all the money he has saved, he moves in and begins planning his next career move.

That very day, however, the local wolf wanders by. Hoping for a supper of "the other white meat," she knocks on the first little pig's door. The pig gets up to answer it, but, remembering all the photos he has seen on milk cartons, he thinks better of it and re-fuses to let the wolf in.

But the wolf doesn't go away. Using deep breathing tech-niques she has learned in her Lamaze classes, she huffs and puffs, over and over, until she finally blows down the straw house. The first little pig manages to run away and save his life, but now he has no house. He vows to purchase adequate homeowner's cover-age in the future.

The second little pig, who attended training in real estate law, has learned that by building a little cottage out of sticks he can avoid having to purchase a construction permit. He puts up

29

his house in just a few days and is pleased with how he has managed to beat the system.

Soon after he moves in, however, the wolf happens by and knocks on the door. "Who is it?" the second little pig asks. "Housing inspector," the wolf says. The second little pig isn't fooled and refuses to let her in.

The wolf remains undaunted, however. Daily workouts on her NordicTrac have made her extremely fit. She inhales deeply and huffs and puffs until the second little pig's house falls apart like an undercapitalized joint venture. The second little pig runs away, barely escaping with his life, and appears on several TV talk shows as a survivor of lupine abuse syndrome.

The third little pig, who attended training in property management, decides to build his house out of bricks. In addition, he installs motion-activated floodlights, video cameras, and an electronic alarm system. When the house is finally finished and the third little pig moves in, he feels safe and secure.

Not long afterward, the wolf pays the third little pig a visit. She pounds on his door, demanding to be let in. "The police have already been notified by my intruder alert system," the third pig informs her via intercom. "They're on their way right now."

But the wolf doesn't give up easily. From her aromatherapy kit, she selects a scent that opens up her lungs. Then she huffs and puffs and huffs and puffs, but this time with no success.

Frustrated and hungry, the wolf climbs up on the roof of the house, slips into the chimney, and begins to slide down. But the third pig moves a pot of water under it and waits nearby, holding a portable hair dryer. When the wolf drops into the pot, the third little pig turns on the hair dryer and tosses it into the water.

There is a huge shower of sparks, and the wolf lets out a terrible howl. She scrambles back up the chimney as fast as she can, and the third little pig gets thirty seconds of coverage on the evening news.

The wolf never comes back, and the third little pig goes on to make a fortune investing in a chain of electrolysis centers.

Basic Lesson

> **Optimal results arise from careful contingency planning.**

Applications for Serious Managers

Most managers do not take contingency planning seriously. Once a direction has been decided on or a major decision has been made, the typical manager fails to consider all the alternative outcomes, let alone chart all the possibilities.

In an effort to save time, effort, and trouble, too many managers plan for only a single outcome. When a different outcome occurs, however, those managers end up jeopardizing their organization's (and their own) future.

Granted, planning for alternative outcomes takes a good deal of time, energy, and money. Had things turned out well for little pigs one and two, they might have felt that contingency planning was wasteful and foolish. But the wise and experienced manager understands that things that work out well tend to do so because of contingency planning, not in spite of it.

The time to chart alternative courses of action is well in advance, before decisions or directions are forced on you by circumstances. This ensures that no matter what happens, at least one of the options and decisions at your disposal will lead to an acceptable outcome.

A Real-World Business "Tale"

A large West Coast hospital was threatened with unionization by its nonprofessional staff. Its housekeepers, engineers, food handlers, and other unlicensed personnel were upset with management because they felt that the hospital's licensed, professional staff received better treatment. These employees contacted the local AFL-CIO, planning both unionization and a strike.

Hospital management was happy to offer its entire staff, both professional and nonprofessional workers, the same standardized benefits and educational leave. However, management was not willing to provide uniforms for all unlicensed personnel and was unwilling to meet all of the nonprofessionals' pay demands.

Although progress was made, the two sides were unable to agree on a settlement. Unionization and a strike seemed more and more inevitable and imminent.

Management decided to create a complete contingency plan. The plan included specific details on how the hospital would stay open even if every single nonprofessional employee joined the strike. In addition, management contacted vendors to make alternative arrangements if unionized vendors such as laundry workers refused to cross the picket line.

The plan was sufficiently detailed, and management was ready to implement it. If the union won the vote and a general strike was called, the hospital would not merely stay open, it could actually run fairly smoothly. As a result, management felt comfortable with its decision to stand firm on its offer of wages and benefits.

Management deliberately left a copy of the complete contingency plan on a copy machine so a union representative could find it. The message to the nonprofessional workers was clear: A strike was no longer a serious threat.

Once this message got around, the nonprofessional staff gave in, accepted management's offer, and did not unionize.

In this case, as in many cases of good contingency planning, being prepared for the worst kept the worst from becoming reality.

The Bottom Line

Contingency planning is a crucial part of any business strategy. This is true for both long-term goals and short-term responses to specific situations.

As long as things go precisely as planned, managers who take shortcuts and avoid contingency planning may appear to save their organizations time and money. But when unexpected or un-welcome events strike and no adequate response has been planned, those same managers may not merely look shortsighted, they may be looking for another job.

Careful contingency planning for unfavorable outcomes is the best way to keep those unfavorable events from occurring.

5. RUMPELSTILTSKIN

Executive Summary

A foolish but highly ambitious entrepreneur brags to the executive director of the Chicago Metals Exchange that he and his daughter have developed a device that turns straw into gold. They have just patented the device, he explains, and infomercials featuring it will begin airing in a few weeks. This claim is a blatant lie, but the entrepreneur hopes to use it to network with several wealthy and important people up until the invention is revealed as a hoax.

The greedy executive director, fearing that the invention will cause the bottom to drop out of the gold market, invites the man and his daughter to dinner at The Drake Hotel. Over dessert, while the father is in the rest room, he issues the daughter an ultimatum: Either she spins him several hundred pounds of gold, which he will sell before the gold market collapses, or he will have his underworld contacts send them both to the bottom of Lake Michigan.

Despairing for her life, the daughter excuses herself to make a phone call. By the coatroom, she encounters a mysterious little man who offers to spin the requisite amount of gold for her. He shows her a device of his own, which closely resembles a Popeil Pocket Fisherman. In exchange, he says, she must give him her newborn child when she becomes a mother. Frantic and desperate, the daughter agrees. A few minutes later, she and her father are loading five hundred pounds of pure gold into the trunk of the executive director's Lincoln.

Years pass. The woman meets a handsome and brilliant MIS director; the two fall in love and soon marry. They settle happily in an apartment on Lake Shore Drive, and a year later she gives birth to a son.

As they are leaving the hospital with their newborn infant, a taxi pulls up beside them. The strange little man gets out and pleasantly but firmly demands the child. "Remember your promise," he says. "The child belongs to me."

Stunned, the woman pleads to be released from their bargain. The little man laughs and says, "Very well. It so happens that I have a very unusual name. If you can guess it within the next forty-eight hours, you may keep the child. Otherwise, he's mine forever." He hands her a business card with nothing on it but an e-mail address. "Go ahead and e-mail me whatever names you can think of. But don't get your hopes up. Nobody's guessed it before." He gets back into the taxi and drives off.

Fortunately, the clever MIS director soon comes up with a plan. Using the network of computers and servers he has created for his employer, he accesses all the databases of past and present names throughout the world, downloads them all onto a single CD-ROM, sorts them by language, and alphabetizes them. Then, using fifteen modems, he sends them all at once to the mysterious little man's e-mail address.

One of the names, Rumpelstiltskin (an Old High German nickname used in western Luxembourg), turns out to be correct. In rage and frustration, the little man sends a surge of electricity back through the system, blowing out all the servers, plus many of the streetlights in Grant Park. But the daughter and her husband get to keep their child, and—except for when the Cubs lose—everyone lives happily ever after.

Basic Lesson

> **Unrealistic performance expectations result in inappropriate behaviors.**

Applications for Serious Managers

It is the responsibility of management to establish the performance goals of its staff. Many managers routinely establish "stretch" goals for their staffs to encourage strong, if not extraordinary, performance. Particularly aggressive managers will stretch those goals even further, sometimes primarily to enhance their own reputations. This has the admirable result of pushing people further and harder than the competition. Yet if people are pushed too far, the outcome can be disastrous.

The challenge, then, becomes determining the fine line between not far enough and too far. Although it may seem that pushing a bit too hard would ensure optimal performance while making management look good, there's a serious downside to this strategy. When pushed to extremes, some staff members may respond with completely inappropriate and unacceptable behavior. Getting out from underneath such unrealistic expectations makes "doing a deal with the devil," or at least a shady character such as Rumpelstiltskin, begin to look at least acceptable, if not downright appealing.

Sales staff facing unattainable quotas attached to future job security may manipulate sales reports and gerrymander year-end records to meet annual goals. Otherwise ethical physicians who feel abused by discounted fee schedules in a beleaguered health care system may feel no guilt about charging for services they didn't provide—or even collecting fees for services to patients they didn't examine. Stockbrokers facing commission thresholds that continuously escalate feel compelled to churn interest in marginally performing companies, regardless of whether those companies have investment potential.

Although no manager wants to encourage such inappropriate behavior, it is understandable how it arises.

A Real-World Business "Tale"

The profits for a well-known athletic shoe company soared for the past three years, with revenue increasing 30 percent a year and bottom-line profits in the double digits. The CEO of this company was thrilled with its performance and wanted it to continue indefinitely.

This year there was a 2 percent decline in revenues in the first quarter. The CEO began to get worried. He assumed the decline was just a matter of laziness. "We've done so well in the past that people just aren't paying attention," he told Jim Rosen, the CFO. He therefore decided that all bonuses for everyone in the company would be paid on an all-or-nothing schedule, with no graduated increments. "We either make our numbers and everyone gets rewarded, or we won't and no one gets anything," he decreed.

When this policy went into effect, the sales quotas were well defined. The quotas were higher than the year before, even though there was a slight decline already, and competition was much more aggressive than in previous years. This did not faze the CEO, however.

Historically, this company had paid large bonuses, but lower-than-average salaries for the industry. Overall, this bonus structure ensured employees higher-than-average incomes. Frontline salespeople all the way up to the executive committee relied on their bonuses in order to meet basic living expenses.

The CEO's new bonus structure motivated the sales force, but no matter how hard the salespeople tried, they couldn't quite reach the new target. After all the numbers were in at the end of the fourth quarter, the company had done well, but had missed its target by about $1 million, which represented just 0.5 percent of total sales revenue.

Jim Rosen regarded such an amount as within the range of a "rounding error" and adjusted the final numbers to come in just a bit above the target. After all, the entire staff was depending on bonuses, and the numbers were never very exact anyway, what with last-minute cancellations, late returns, delayed payments, and so on.

The CEO was thrilled that the company had reached its target and was sure that the cause was his aggressive new bonus policy. "No graduated bonus payments," he said. "It's all or nothing again next year." The CEO also increased the targets once again.

The next year a similar scenario occurred. This time, however, CFO Jim Rosen had to creatively account for a $3.5 million difference at the end of the year. To do so, Jim had to include two other senior executives in his manipulation of the books.

This situation continued to escalate each year, with the CEO setting ever more unattainable targets and the CFO becoming more and more creative in his accounting.

Finally, after five years, the company's accounting firm went to the board of directors to inform them that the company was close to insolvency.

The unrealistic goals, and the all-or-nothing bonus structure based on these goals, resulted in the downfall of a $200 million company and jail terms for several of its top executives.

The Bottom Line

Management is responsible for encouraging staff performance. It is also responsible for keeping goals reasonable, appropriate, and realistic. When a harmless animal is backed into a corner, a natural reflex for self-preservation makes it turn vicious. In similar fashion, when backed into a corner, an otherwise talented and committed employee may become dysfunctional, causing irreparable damage to a company.

The qualified manager sets expectations for both performance and behavior, then from experience establishes acceptable limits for each.

6. THE EMPEROR'S NEW CLOTHES

Executive Summary

he Emperor of a tiny principality is a self-admitted slave to fashion. His robes are by Isaac Mizrahi, his crown is by Halston, and his custom-designed suits bear the labels of other top fashion designers. He even commissioned Anne Klein to create a special cologne, known as His Highness, which he alone is permitted to wear (though close imitations are widely available from street vendors).

One day the Emperor's minister of commerce informs him that a new clothing manufacturer is considering incorporating in the principality because of its minimal taxes and low wages for blue-collar labor. The owners, his minister tells him, are two of the most highly touted young fashion designers in the world, having recently wowed audiences in Paris, Milan, and Tokyo.

Intrigued, the Emperor invites the owners to dinner at the palace. Over their veal piccata, the designers—one Dashe von Habermas from Denmark and one Sheldon de la Feldman from New York—take the Emperor into their confidence. "Your taste, sire, is impeccable," de la Feldman tells him. "But the materials you've been wearing are a tad gauche."

"Outmoded," echoes von Habermas. "Outré. Tacky. You might as well be wearing a Kevlar jumpsuit."

"I don't understand," the Emperor says. "I use only the finest imported silks, cottons, and cashmere."

De la Feldman shakes his head. "Your highness," he says sadly, "we dispensed with natural fibers two seasons ago, once we found a reliable source of Spinlight."

"Spinlight?" the Emperor says. "I've never heard of it before."

Von Habermas widens his eyes. "I'm surprised, sire, that someone as worldly as your highness would fail to keep up on all the developments in fiber optics. Spinlight is made of the same material as transcontinental phone lines, only much finer. It refracts the full spectrum of light in a wonderfully flattering manner, yet it's so lightweight that you can scarcely feel it. Most of what we're creating for our new London show is made from it."

"Unfortunately, it's immensely expensive," confesses de la Feldman. "And the fibers are so fine and delicate that people who lack taste or intelligence are unable to see them at all—also people who are unfit for their jobs or who have reached their level of incompetence."

The Emperor stands up and touches de la Feldman on the shoulder with his Bill Blass scepter. "I hereby commission you and your partner to create for me new royal robes made entirely of Spinlight. Cost is not an issue."

"Your highness," von Habermas says humbly, "we accept the commission."

For weeks the two designers labor in seclusion—though for doing the actual cutting and sewing, they set up an impromptu sweatshop and hire foreign-born workers. During this time, von Habermas and de la Feldman purchase substantial quantities of Spinlight, which FedEx delivers from Silicon Valley in large crates. (These boxes appear to uncultured observers to be empty.) They also consume a great deal of fine wine and rich food.

Finally, the day arrives when the robes are ready. At a preliminary fitting, the Emperor is initially perplexed, for he has difficulty seeing or feeling the clothes at all. But his countenance brightens significantly when his royal advisers compliment the designers on the style, color, cut, and fit of his ultralightweight attire. Relying as usual on the judgment of his council, he limits his suggestions to minor folds and inconsequential tucks. He pays the designers their fee of a half-million dollars, plus expenses, and commands the completion of all refinements by the following morning.

The next day, the cunning designers pantomime the ritual dressing of the Emperor in his newly crafted robes. To show their gratitude, they also present him with a complete set of royal undergarments made of Spinlight at no additional cost.

Then the Emperor sets forth to present his perfectly attired imperial figure to the populace, whose taxes have made it all possible. As he parades through the admiring crowd, which is already quite familiar with the remarkable qualities of the new robes, praise and admiration spring forth from all sides.

Then a well-known consumer advocate steps out of the throng. His own clothes are rumpled and worn, and he wears unflattering black spectacles. "Sire," he says firmly, "as head of the principality's branch of National Public Interest Research Groups, it's my obligation to point out to you and your subjects that you're naked. You've been the victim of the country's worst case of consumer fraud in over a decade."

Outraged, the Emperor flees back to his palace and orders the designers arrested. But by then the designers are already on a plane for Marseilles. They are the ones who live happily ever after.

Basic Lesson

Individuals without a vested interest are the only reliable sources of accurate information.

Applications for Serious Managers

While the issue of conflict of interest is intuitively obvious, it is frequently ignored in the realm of business. Wall Street analysts routinely tout stocks that their employers (through different divisions) have introduced into the market with initial public offerings (IPOs). Management consultants are hired to address issues that, if they were ever actually resolved, would eliminate the need for management consultants. Clinical researchers herald the benefits of the latest medical technology or pharmaceutical breakthrough; only later do we learn that they hold a stock position in the company that sells it and that their research was funded by this same organization. A morass of vested interests lies just beneath the veneer of much of business propriety.

Unless you can be assured of the genuine objectivity of your source, all bets should be off regarding the value of the information or the credibility of any recommendation you receive. When corporate board members hold large stock or option positions in the organization, unless that incentive structure is clearly understood, their decisions may turn out to be more beneficial to their own short-term interests, rather than to the longer-term concerns of the majority of investors.

We all want to believe in well-respected, properly credentialed sources of information. But in our need to trust the experts, we may ignore what is obvious in favor of what we hope to see. Meanwhile, the brave and clear-sighted "innocent" in an organization—the one who "calls 'em like he sees 'em"—may be ignored, or at least viewed as hopelessly naive.

Only later, buck naked in the glare of public scrutiny like the Emperor or buffeted in the windstorm of saner reevaluations, do we appreciate the magnitude of our self-deception.

The only consistently reliable source for screening the information and recommendations you receive is the fine-meshed filter of your visceral response. Ask not who is telling you something, but rather why they are telling it to you at all. What do "expert sources" have to gain by your acceptance of their contribution or advice? If the answer is absolutely nothing (other than having objectively fulfilled your needs), then perhaps you can rely on what you have learned from them.

On the other hand, if you can identify what they have to gain from your acceptance of their ideas or recommendations, you had better carefully evaluate what you and your organization have to lose from doing what they suggest.

A Real-World Business "Tale"

A handful of ex-Microsoft executives set up a software development firm in Bellevue, Washington. The company began marketing a networking product, which quickly became popular.

Each of the four founding principals handled a corporate division. While research and development, sales and marketing, and manufacturing and quality control were well run, the customer support division, handled by principal Kevin Breedlove, was plagued with complaints about access problems and delayed response times.

Kevin was intimately familiar with the company's product and knew that its superb documentation resolved most customers' problems once they were linked with the correct database. However, for months the problem of customers being unable to easily access support services by phone or modem had become steadily worse. Call-waiting times were long and getting longer; call abandonment rates were increasing exponentially; and the success of the entire company was being jeopardized by a rumor that its customer service was seriously flawed and the bugs could not be exterminated.

While the whole organization was concerned about resolving the access issue, it was Kevin's responsibility to implement the action plan. Three times in as many months, the troubleshooting unit from the company's long-distance carrier sent a team to evaluate the problem. Each time, Kevin responded to their recommendations—first with an upgrade of the call-distribution switches, then with additional staff and flexible hours to handle the peak demand periods, and finally with more expensive phones with extra features and added extensions. Yet the problem had only grown worse as the popularity and market penetration of the company's innovative product further stressed the tenuous system with more and more calls.

Under pressure from his partners to fix the problem yesterday, Kevin brought in an independent group of communications consultants for a second opinion on potential solutions to the access dilemma. The ink was barely dry on the fixed-price consulting agreement when the consultants revealed the problem to be not an internal one, but rather a natural result of the outmoded central switching equipment used regionally by the long-distance carrier. Kevin's original due diligence in selecting the carrier had not detected this red flag because all the references he had checked were customers in different regions—regions that already had updated equipment.

The consulting community was quite familiar with the carrier Kevin had selected and knew that his organization's problems were a common occurrence for other carrier customers as well. These problems were not going to be resolved with anything short of an expensive equipment upgrade that the carrier had budgeted for next year. In the meantime, the customers of Kevin's company could only be placated with costly (and largely cosmetic) "solutions" to buy time.

The consultants reviewed the carrier's service agreement and were able to establish that the equipment in use did not meet the contract specifications. The carrier's refund—in lieu of a lawsuit and considerable bad publicity—helped to pay for the next consulting project, which was to select a carrier with adequate equipment to meet customer demand. Still, it took the sales and marketing division almost eighteen months to get past the sales slump, while the company lost market share to its major competitor.

The Bottom Line

Knowledge and information are power. Deceptive information can therefore render you powerless.

Your source of information is a serious consideration. Even if the information you need is available through opinion polls or simple library research, the "emperor's error" suggests that the outcomes may be entirely predictable ahead of time, once you have determined who gathered the information or funded the project.

Prudent managers weigh the source of any information received and act with a commitment commensurate with their instinct for its reliability. To do otherwise is to run the risk of a very public embarrassment.

7. THE LITTLE MATCH GIRL

Executive Summary

he Little Match Girl (LMG) lives in poverty with her entrepreneurial, risk-taking parents. Over the years they have tried many different businesses, all of them failures, has have left them with substantial debts on their failed investments.

However, both of LMG's parents are scrappy, type A people who never give up. In fact, they have already begun start-up on their newest venture, which they are sure will quickly reverse their fortunes. The new business involves selling cheap knockoffs of famous brand-name lighters to passersby on busy street corners in Los Angeles.

LMG's waiflike appearance, while not quite rivaling that of Kate Moss, qualifies her as head of marketing for the operation. Admittedly, it is a department of one, but this gives her the flexibility to set her own sales goals, target her own customers, and develop her own marketing strategies, unencumbered by micromanagement from parental leadership. (It also allows her to immediately bestow upon herself the title of Marketing Employee of the Month.)

The new business's fiscal year begins on January 1, so her first day of business is New Year's Day. Although LMG's marketing plan does not include work on national holidays, she understands the need for aggressive positioning and a high profile in any start-up operation. So LMG takes the bus into Los Angeles, targets a desirable-looking street corner, and starts peddling her lighters outside a bar.

Unfortunately, she finds the streets nearly deserted and the weather unseasonably cool. Furthermore, the California legislature recently banned smoking in bars, which means that many of her potential customers turn out to be nonsmokers.

Not only that, but after a half-hour El Niño rears its ugly head and it starts raining. Fat, heavy raindrops pour down on LMG, and soon she is so wet and cold that she has to warm herself with the flame of one of her lighters.

She holds the cheap imitation close to her face and stares into the tiny flame. The warmth feels good on her face and the propane fumes make her light-headed.

In the glow of the dancing flame, she envisions a more profitable business in a better-researched marketplace. She imagines a more carefully developed business plan, more job security, fully vested stock options, and a 401(k) pension program. Huddled there on the street corner over the tiny flame, she immerses herself in this comforting illusion until the cylinder is drained of its fuel.

She wrings the water out of her hair, flicks open another lighter, and continues her daydreaming. This time she imagines a profit-sharing plan, flex time, regular trips to professional conferences, and rapid promotion to the position of senior vice president. Eventually she lets her thoughts wander into a fantasy in which she sits at the helm of a multinational conglomerate offering a variety of flame-producing devices, from lighters to acetylene torches to rocket engines.

So entranced is LMG in these visions that she forgets the time, the task at hand, and the temperature. She sits on the ground and continues to light each and every lighter until she has used up her entire inventory—all without selling a single unit.

It is almost midnight. She is frightened to go home and tell her parents about the unintentional liquidation of her entire stock. Since she has missed her last bus anyway, she decides to spend the night under a freeway overpass.

Sadly, LMG is never seen or heard from again. The next day, police find a trail of empty, discarded lighters leading from beneath the overpass to an odd circle of stones near a corn canning plant. Although police presume that LMG was washed away by a flash flood caused later that night by El Niño, some people—mostly X-Files groupies—believe aliens (who, they claim, have a deep interest in miniature propane tanks) abducted her. LMG's parents grieve over her disappearance for several weeks, then at last make their fortune importing poly/nylon mittens produced in third-world sweatshops.

Basic Lesson

> **Inadequate business planning results in business failure.**

Applications for Serious Managers

The creation of a solid and well-thought-out business plan is critical for any successful business endeavor. Large corporations routinely hire large consulting firms to help them develop their business plans; unfortunately, many small, entrepreneurial companies fail to invest in this same process.

Indeed, if no outside capital is needed for the business, the small business owner will have no external motivation to create a solid business plan. In fact, small business owners may see the written business plan as a burdensome process. This is, to put it quite mildly, a huge mistake.

An effective business plan should clearly define the goals and objectives of the company; allocate sufficient resources for the organization's development and success; define and clarify responsibility and accountability at all levels; and provide for periodic monitoring and feedback mechanisms as the company grows.

The specific components of a good business plan include:

* A description of the business and its future potential
* An outline of its management structure
* A description of the financing
* A list of risk factors and competitors
* An analysis of likely return on investment
* Potential exit strategies
* An analysis of operations and projections
* Financial statements
* Financial projections
* Product literature, brochures, articles, illustrations, and other collateral materials

The Little Match Girl's business of selling cheesy lighters on the street corner was doomed from the beginning. The family business (and probably the Little Match Girl herself) was done in by inadequate preparation, poor market analysis, a burdensome regulatory environment, inappropriate marketing strategies, and unseasonable weather.

With a little business planning, LMG's parents would have quickly realized that selling lighters on the streets of California would not meet either their short-term or long-term business objectives.

A Real-World Business "Tale"

A husband and wife team decided to go into the flag business, selling decorative flags at an outdoor swap meet in south Florida every Sunday. The swap meet took place year-round and always seemed to be very busy. Furthermore, decorative flags seemed to be appearing on more and more homes, so they knew there was a ready market for the product.

The couple decided to invest about $10,000 in the venture, but never did any formal business planning before they made their investment and opened their stand.

When the couple approached the swap-meet owners, they were given a fairly good location. To keep this location, they decided to pay in advance for an entire year. However, they never thought to ask for the exclusive right to sell flags at the swap meet, and within four weeks there were two other vendors selling flags. As the weeks passed, other problems emerged as well. They quickly discovered that they had grossly underestimated the time needed to set up and tear down their stand each Sunday. They had sloppy inventory control, so often they had too many of some designs and not enough of others. And since they had never attempted to calculate the actual costs of doing business, at the end of one year the couple discovered that they were making less than minimum wage.

They then tried to sell the business, but the flag craze was all but over and by now discount stores such as Kmart and Target were selling the same flags for less. Finally, just to get out of the business, they gave away the flags to local charities and used the loss as a tax deduction.

The Bottom Line

Business plans serve a definite purpose and can assist anyone in the advance evaluation of the potential success of any business. The discipline of putting information down on paper and identifying the positive and negatives of a business before the business is started can be invaluable. It can also prevent a great deal of future aggravation and hardship.

A fancy, fifty-page business plan isn't necessary for a small business. Nevertheless, to avoid the "Little Match Girl's mistake," it is crucial to put the basics of any new business on paper before it gets rolling. Otherwise, the business could go up in flames all too quickly.

8. HANSEL AND GRETEL

Executive Summary

ansel and Gretel live in a custom-designed cottage deep in the California woods. They are able to have this standard of living because their father and stepmother own a successful home business, Log On, which sells firewood over the Internet.

Hansel and Gretel are sad and scrawny children because their stepmother feeds them nothing but fresh, raw fruits and vegetables. "If you eat the right foods in the right combinations," their stepmom assures them, "you'll grow up to have perfect bodies and attitudes. Then you'll be ideally positioned to take over our business, and you can continue to live way out here in the wilderness, working sixteen hours a day for the sheer joy of it, just like us." Hansel and Gretel would prefer part-time minimum wage jobs as product testers in an Oreo factory, but they know better than to say anything.

One night, as they are falling asleep, Hansel and Gretel overhear their father and stepmother talking in the next room. "I think we need to downsize the family," their stepmom says. "The kids are becoming less and less cost-effective. Look at this graph I put together. There's virtually no ROI, and their cuteness indicators are way down. If we offer them a severance package, we can reduce headcount by 50 percent."

"Maybe you should look at your own pie chart," they hear their father reply. "It shows that you're 36 percent selfish, 41 percent hard-hearted, and 23 percent off your authentic bentwood rocker. Now please go to sleep."

The next morning their stepmother invites Hansel and Gretel to join her for a walk. They agree, and she leads them deep into the forest, to a place that is dark and unfamiliar. "Where are we going?" Gretel asks, worried.

"They finally opened a Gap out here," the stepmother replies. "And an Orange Julius. They're just a little farther on."

"I'm really tired," Gretel says.

"You two wait here," says their stepmother. "I'll run ahead and get us all something to drink." The children sit down tiredly, and the stepmother disappears into the forest.

"She's terminating us, isn't she?" Gretel asked.

"Uh-huh," replies Hansel. "She's our own personal Chainsaw Alice."

"What do we do now? We'll never find our way home. It's starting to get dark."

"See that light way off in the distance? Maybe it's somebody's house," says Hansel. "Let's go see."

Slowly and wearily, Hansel and Gretel make their way toward the light.

"What is it?" Hansel asks as they draw near. "It looks like some kind of cheesy discount store."

Gretel peers into the gloom, reading the neon sign. "Sweetness'n Lite Candy Outlet Mall. Public welcome."

Hand in hand, they creep nearer until they are close enough to touch the building.

"The construction looks really shoddy," Hansel says. He reaches out and pulls off a handful of siding. "Hey, it's made of gingerbread. And look—the awnings are giant chocolate bars. And the bricks in the walkway are biscotti. Boy, the housing inspector's going to have a fit."

Suddenly the door to the building opens, and an old woman comes hobbling out. "Ah, cheap labor!" she cackles to herself. "Good evening, children! Are you responding to the ad for dynamic, people-oriented individuals interested in pursuing an exciting management opportunity with a fast-paced, growing retail sales organization?"

"No," Hansel replies. "But we are a couple of kids that need work and will accept lots of candy, minimum wage, and no benefits."

"Bingo. You also get all the junk food you can eat, drink, or steal when I'm not looking."

"It's a deal," says Gretel.

So Hansel and Gretel go to work for Sweetness'n Lite (a division of Multichem Labs, Inc.). The pay is poor and their jobs are dull, and before long each of them has put on twenty pounds and developed a serious case of acne. But they are happy not to have to eat healthy food all the time—and not to have to deal with their obnoxious stepmother anymore. Still, they miss their dad and their old home, and sometimes they wish they were back with their family again.

Then, early one morning, a strange man in a lab coat shows up from corporate headquarters. "So, how are you kids doing?" he asks. "Feeling pretty good?"

"No," says Gretel. "I get headaches and dizzy spells from eating so much sugar."

"And I've become alternately hyperactive and lethargic," says Hansel.

The man nods. "At Multichem Labs, we've developed a wonderful new pill that can alleviate all those symptoms—and help you lose weight, to boot. It's very expensive, but that won't matter if you have health insurance, which unfortunately you don't."

"Wait a minute!" Gretel shouts, jumping to her feet. "Now I understand! You've been dumping all this low-grade candy on the market at rock-bottom prices just to fatten people up. Then you move in for the kill by selling them a drug to help them handle all the crapola they've been eating."

The man beams at Gretel. "Sweetie, you are sharp! You're management material if I ever saw it. I'm going to get you signed up for Multichem's leadership training program."

"No!" shout Hansel and Gretel together. They push the man into a trough full of Gummi Bears, then go running out into the forest. They continue to run all day until they can run no more, and they sink wearily to the ground.

"Hey," says Hansel. "Isn't that the road to our house?"

They leap up again and follow the road to their home, where they reunite joyfully with their father, who serves them a delicious dinner of tomato soup and macaroni and cheese. "When your stepmom ran off with a man who runs an online psychic business," he explains, "I was free to go back to eating regular food." He wipes a tear from his eye. "I'm so glad you kids are home again. Want to celebrate with a vacation in L.A.?"

Basic Lesson

> **If something appears too good to be true, it usually is.**

Applications for Serious Managers

All of us have been faced with an offer that seems too wonderful to be real, yet many of us nevertheless accept that offer without too much questioning, just as Hansel and Gretel did at Sweetness'n Lite. Whether we are presented with a potential purchase that is priced well below market value, a job that doubles our current salary, or a contract that gives us everything we asked for, we tend to overlook the obvious—there is no free lunch.

In Hansel and Gretel's case, the seemingly free lunch turned out to be fattening, unhealthy, and ultimately a setup for exploitation. This arrangement appears over and over in corporate life, under a variety of guises. The outcome, however, is almost always the same: What looked like a great deal in the short run turns out to be a poor one over the long term.

Success in business—or in any type of negotiation—occurs only when each party achieves some or all of its objectives. Give and take, compromise and balance are necessary ingredients in any deal or negotiation. No party ever wins or loses completely. Therefore, if you think that you have gotten everything you asked for (or more), be suspicious.

Take the time to learn as much as you can about the company, job, service, or product under discussion. Read contracts carefully. Check references, from both happy and unhappy customers. Talk to line employees of the company, rather than taking the word of the sales force, who are paid to sell. Check out the company's products; if appropriate, visit customers.

If you discover that things are not what they seem, you'll have made that discovery early enough to disengage without much difficulty. And if what you discover results in a somewhat less rosy picture, but one that's attractive nevertheless, then you're able to proceed with clearer vision and greater confidence. Either way, you're able to make your decision based on how things actually are, rather than how you hope they'll be—or how others are presenting them to you.

A Real-World Business "Tale"

Ed Cochran was a mechanic at Sandy's Import Specialists. He was highly skilled, and after working at Sandy's for three years, he received Automotive Service Excellence (ASE) certification in engine performance, brakes, and advanced engine repair. Ed was extremely reliable, never calling in sick and often being the first to volunteer for additional hours. Although Ed was newly married, he did not mind working on weekends or late at night. His reliability, flexibility, and ASE certification made him an extremely attractive employee.

Ed's reputation as an excellent mechanic spread, and soon he was offered a job at a nearby competitor, Fairmont Auto. Fairmont offered Ed $50 more per week in guaranteed salary and promised him a 26 percent commission on all work he performed. Fairmont's owner, Scott Lanier, told Ed that he could earn an enormous amount in commissions at Fairmont. "In fact," Lanier said, "it's quite common for our mechanics to make almost as much just in commission as you're making in salary right now." Ed was excited by the offer and eagerly accepted the new job.

But before he told the people at Sandy's that he was leaving, Ed mentioned the job change to his new in-laws. It sounded too good to be true to his father-in-law, who suggested to Ed that he talk with some of the other mechanics at Fairmont.

Thinking this was a good idea, Ed took several of Fairmont's mechanics to lunch. In that one-hour lunch, he found out three important things. First, the 26 percent commission would be applied against his salary, which meant that he wouldn't see anything over and above his salary unless he worked at a frantic speed. Second, this bait-and-switch technique was typical of how Fairmont's owner treated its mechanics. Third, and not surprisingly, turnover at Fairmont was high, and actually two of the men sitting at Ed's restaurant table were looking for new jobs.

Ed decided that the $50 weekly difference in salary was not worth being treated badly by his employer. He also decided that he was overdue for a significant raise from Sandy's. Using the offer from Fairmont as leverage, Ed was able to negotiate a salary increase of $70 a week to stay at Sandy's. And when he received his first enhanced paycheck, Ed celebrated by taking his wife and in-laws to dinner.

The Bottom Line

Whether we're being misled or simply letting our hopes get the best of us, it can be dangerous to say yes to any offer too quickly.

Good deals are not inherently fraudulent, although they typically are not as wonderful as they initially seem or have a downside that isn't immediately obvious. But in our eagerness to reap the benefits or rewards we desire, we may skip the crucial step of acquiring the detailed information we need to make a truly informed decision.

We must remember to investigate things thoroughly before signing on the dotted line, no matter what carrots are dangled on a stick before us. For, unlike Hansel and Gretel, we (and our organizations) do not have the option of bailing out and running home to papa.

9. THE TWELVE DANCING PRINCESSES

Executive Summary

A king has twelve attractive teenage daughters. He is naturally worried about their moral development, since just about every male in the kingdom would be happy to make love to any of them.

To keep an eye on all twelve daughters, the king insists that they all share a single giant bedroom (and one very large bathroom) on the top floor of his castle. As an extra precaution, he has their bedroom door locked and bolted from the outside each night so that he will always know where they are.

Soon after his oldest daughter's seventeenth birthday, a maid reports something strange. Each morning, she says, the soles of all the girls' sandals are almost completely worn away. Each day the maid has replaced them with new ones from the royal shoemaker's stock, but now there are only about twenty pairs left in the shoemaker's inventory. The maid says humbly, "I'm worried, sire. A pair of sandals should last longer than a single night."

The king thinks it odd, too, so he confronts his two oldest daughters and asks them about the sandals.

"Elves," says the sixteen-year-old. "Or maybe wizardry. Someone evil probably cast a spell on all our footwear."

"Why would anyone do that?" the king wants to know.

"For heaven's sake, daddy," the oldest daughter says, tossing her hair impatiently. "We live in a small medieval country. The

65

whole kingdom's crawling with elves and trolls and wizards and warlocks. Remember the time mommy got turned into a serpent for a week? Anyway, if you'd get us some decent Birkenstocks instead of those cheesy royal shoemaker things, maybe they'd last a little longer."

The king is not convinced. He decides to put an ad in the *Kingdom Shopping News* stating that any man who discovers what happens to his daughters each night may choose one of them as his bride. But any man who tries and fails will have to become one of the king's servants for life.

Around this time, a disabled and destitute soldier arrives in the capital. He has been a failure in his original position as a soldier, having not only lost the battle, but gotten wounded as well. He has come to the city hoping to make a career switch, ideally to a position with long-term potential in a service business. He is willing to work very hard—but as he quickly learns, the kingdom has no disability policy and, as a result, no one will hire him.

After getting turned away by every employer in town, the soldier finally limps to the castle to volunteer, anticipating a life as one of the king's servants. It isn't his career of choice by any means, but at least he'll have food and a bed—and although it is an entry-level position, it is with the kingdom's most stable and prosperous employer.

"I'm here about the ad," the soldier says to the castle gatekeeper.

"Sorry," the gatekeeper replies. "The mule's already been sold."

"No, the other ad."

"Oh, the PI job. Sure, sign here." He unfolds a piece of parchment and hands the solider a lump of charcoal, which the soldier uses to sign his name. "Okay," the guard says, "you're hired. Here's a spyglass and there's the tower where the girls live. No admittance to the castle and its grounds—after all, you're just a peasant. You have two fortnights to solve the mystery. On day twenty-nine, report for duty as a stableboy."

That night, as the poor soldier wanders through the forest, limping and shivering, he comes upon a sweet-looking elderly woman. "You look sad, bubbeleh," the woman says. "What's wrong?" The soldier tells her the whole story, and the woman—who, like most strangers in the woods in those days, is actually a fairy—takes pity on him. "Enough, already!" she says. "You want I should sit here crying my eyes out all night? Here, take my cloak. It's just a schmata—it's not mink or anything—but it'll keep you warm. Also, it makes you invisible."

"Really?" the soldier asks.

"Sure, unless you're wearing glasses or dressed in armor. It's designed for avoiding trolls and casting spells without being seen. But I also use it for getting the best view at jousting events, sneaking into royal weddings, that sort of thing. Anyway, it's yours. Just remember—bathe first and keep your mouth shut. Being invisible does bupkiss for smells and sounds."

The soldier thanks the old woman and hurries back to the castle.

Early the next evening the soldier bathes thoroughly in the stream, then dresses himself in the cloak. Immediately he becomes invisible. Slowly, so as not to make noise, he creeps past the palace guards, up the stairs, and into the girls' bedroom. He climbs up into the rafters, gets comfortable, and waits.

Not too long after supper, a maid lets all twelve of the girls into the room and helps them get ready for bed. When they are all tucked under the covers, the maid leaves, locking and bolting the door behind her.

After a few minutes of silence the youngest girl whispers, "Now?"

"Now!" the oldest whispers back.

All twelve girls throw back their covers and leap from their beds. Hurriedly, they dress and put on their sandals. Then they slide aside a panel in the back of a closet. Behind it is a secret stairway, which they all hurry down. The soldier follows a discreet distance behind.

The stairs lead to a secret ballroom in the castle's sub-basement, where there wait twelve enchanted dancing instructors—each one young, handsome, well-dressed, and (as the soldier quickly discovers) very gay. Throughout the night, they lead the twelve daughters through one dance step after another: the waltz, tango, fox-trot, two-step, polka, Charleston, macarena, twist, lambada, bunny hop, limbo, hokeypokey, and the mashed potato. The soldier sees that all twelve daughters have become accomplished dancers.

Since he is invisible, he tries out some of the steps himself, alone in the corner. To his delight, he discovers that despite his limp, he can waltz and two-step very presentably.

When the first rooster crows just before dawn, the twelve dance instructors kiss the twelve daughters on their foreheads and bow. "You're all angels," one of them says. "If I were straight, I'd slay dragons all night for any one of you, no questions asked. Now go back upstairs and get an hour of sleep. And for Pete's sake, girls, get your father to buy you some decent sandals."

The next morning the soldier reports his findings to the royal court. The king is relieved and delighted to know that no one has been taking advantage of his daughters—and that they are learning something artistic, to boot. He knights the twelve dance instructors, which amuses them greatly, since, being enchanted, they hardly need any royal perks. He gives the soldier the title of Sir Thomas and the lifelong appointment of Director of Investigative Affairs for His Majesty's Court, as well as a hefty salary. And, by and by, the ex-soldier and the oldest daughter—who is also the best dancer—fall in love, marry, and live long and happy lives together.

As for the magic cloak, Sir Thomas soon learns to use it for dozens of helpful purposes, from sneaking behind enemy lines to fighting crime to secretly kissing the back of his wife's neck in public.

Basic Lesson

> **Specific technology from one industry can be successfully adapted to others.**

Applications for Serious Managers

Adapting technology from one industry to another can be critical—in part because of the enormous savings in research and development costs, in part because of the great reduction in time in bringing a new product to market. If the soldier had had to invent a cloak that would make him invisible, he would have been an old man before discovering the secret of the dancing shoes. By using the technology of the cloak given to him by the elderly woman in the woods, he was able to solve the mystery and marry a princess.

The classic example of such adaptation is the laser. Very quickly after its development in the early 1960s, scientists began redesigning lasers for military purposes. Almost simultaneously, laser technology was adapted for use in drilling, cutting, and welding. The aerospace industry soon developed a variety of new uses for the technology, and each passing year has brought further developments and products. Lasers are now widely used for surgery, touch verification systems, security systems, and data storage and retrieval. Home computers, CD-ROM players, and DVD players all rely on laser technology. Our global network of sophisticated communications systems would be impossible without the laser. The laser could never have advanced so far or so quickly without the widespread willingness of many industries to adapt existing technology for their own purposes. As a result, the laser became widely used in military, industrial, and consumer settings in a relatively short time.

A Real-World Business "Tale"

Dr. Thomas Whitmore was a successful ophthalmologist living in southern California. His office was close to a large senior housing project, in which many of his clients lived. For nearly two decades Dr. Whitmore enjoyed a virtual monopoly in the neighborhood. He had performed many hundreds of cataract operations, all of which were profitable, and he expected to perform many more. At age sixty-one, Dr. Whitmore had plans to work four more years, then retire. Now, for the first time, Dr. Whitmore suddenly was facing some serious competition.

Dr. Lin Chow, who had recently completed his ophthalmology residency program, decided to open his new practice only a block away. Dr. Chow did a great deal of initial marketing, putting ads in the city and neighborhood newspapers and mailing brochures to everyone in the neighborhood—including every resident of the senior housing project. In these ads, Dr. Chow stressed the benefits of laser surgery, a service that Dr. Whitmore did not offer and had not been trained in.

As a result of these ads, Dr. Chow managed to pick up about 10 percent of Dr. Whitmore's clientele. Most of the neighborhood's seniors, however, continued to use Dr. Whitmore—partly because he was competent and friendly, partly because they were accustomed to him.

One afternoon, one of Dr. Whitmore's long-term patients, Sophie Markowitz, showed up for an emergency visit. Dr. Whitmore quickly determined that she had a retinal hemorrhage, so he admitted her to the local hospital, where he performed a buckle procedure on her eye. Although the procedure was successful, it required Sophie to remain in the hospital for three days. During those three days, through no fault of Dr. Whitmore's, a great deal went wrong. The hospital food did not agree with her, so her stomach was often upset. On the second day she fell out of bed and sprained her wrist. Finally, just before she was to be discharged, the hospital's computers went down; she was told that she couldn't leave until her final paperwork had been generated, and she was made to wait for well over an hour. Sophie was understandably upset by the entire experience.

A few days afterward, another resident from the senior project, Antonio Furia, also experienced a retinal hemorrhage. He went to Dr. Chow, who used a laser to coagulate the hemorrhage and stop the bleeding. Antonio's procedure was done in the hospital's ambulatory surgery center, and he was able to return home the same day. He had no complications and could hardly believe how easy the surgery was.

Both seniors told other residents in the project about their experiences. Word spread quickly, and before long many of the seniors began making appointments with Dr. Chow. By the time Dr. Chow had been in business for fourteen months, he was so busy that he brought in a partner who was also skilled in performing laser surgery.

Dr. Whitmore, on the other hand, soon was working only two days a week. Ultimately, he retired from his practice two years earlier than planned.

The Bottom Line

Adapting technology from one industry to another can be critical to a business's survival, particularly in highly competitive fields. Contrary to popular belief, this technology does not always have to take the form of expensive equipment. In some cases it may be a new process or design. In others, a new technology can be decidedly low tech and inexpensive. Consider the person who observed the beverage holders installed in seats in theaters and stadiums and decided to adapt them to automobiles and minivans.

To maintain market share, a business needs to be constantly on the lookout for new ways to use technology. It also needs to be ready and willing to adapt it in a timely manner. This may require not only the purchase of new technology, but also the training or retraining of personnel as well. Nevertheless, the investment can often make the difference between viability or failure for a business.

10. SLEEPING BEAUTY

Executive Summary

rich and Marlene Somnolenz are two of the world's wealthiest and most glamorous people. Erich is CEO of Somnoco, one of America's most profitable family-owned businesses; Marlene is a direct descendent of the royal family of Luxembourg. They live in La Jolla, where they throw world-renowned parties and dabble in assorted New Age practices.

After being childless for many years, Erich and Marlene are at last able to conceive with the help of a crystal healer, a high-fertility diet, and San Diego's most exclusive fertility clinic. To their delight, a beautiful blonde, blue-eyed child is born nine months later. After considering Faith, Hope, Charity, Grace, Prudence, and Irene, they finally decide on the name Venus.

In honor of their newborn baby, the couple decides to throw their most gala event ever—a "celebration of new life." Guests include the world's most prominent channelers, healers, psychotherapists, relationship counselors, shamans, body workers, and spirit guides.

Not invited, however, is John Gold, author of the best-selling books *Affirmations to Make Yourself Perfect* and *Money: Your Key to Enlightenment*. Gold is a pleasant fellow, and the Somnolenzes had planned to have him serve as master of ceremonies for the event, but Bucky, the astral being whom Gold channels, is often rude. (At Erich and Marlene's last party, Bucky called them "self-indulgent, San Pellagrino–swilling dilettantes.") Their fear of

Bucky's harsh tongue ultimately causes them to leave Gold (and Bucky) off the guest list.

Gold doesn't mind not being invited, but Bucky is incensed. So, when Gold contacts Bucky on the evening of the party, Bucky quickly takes over his body. He drives Gold's car to the Somnolenz home, gets past security guards by pretending to be the astral teacher Seth, and makes his way to the center of the family ballroom, where Venus is on display in her crib.

Bucky leans over the crib and puts his hand on the baby's forehead. "Listen carefully," he says to her. "Nothing worldly will ever satisfy you. All this wealth is going to bore you, enervate you, exhaust you. It'll all seem so tawdry and meaningless that you won't be able to stay awake." He removes his hand and sneaks out.

As the years pass and Venus grows up, she remains as beautiful as ever. But when she reaches young adulthood, she mysteriously becomes more and more tired. When she is in the presence of her parents, her eyes soon begin to droop, and when she attends parties or other high-society gatherings, she falls fast asleep within minutes.

Frightened, Marlene and Erich escort her to the best and most expensive healers they can find. "Chronic fatigue syndrome," says a famous neurologist. "Epstein-Barr," says the author of *Buy This Book and Live Forever*. "Narcolepsy," says a world-renowned naturopath. "Depression," says a prominent therapist who has appeared on *Oprah*. "A posthypnotic suggestion planted at an early age," says a highly respected psychic. "An energy block in the heart chakra," speculates a tai chi master. "She's a spoiled brat who's been given everything but challenges," explains a psychologist who has her own talk show.

Erich and Marlene pay top dollar for every possible diagnosis and cure, yet nothing any of the expensive healers do is of any help. Venus sleeps more and more, until she lapses into a near-coma, rising only to eat, bathe, and use the bathroom.

Then, after Venus has slept almost constantly for exactly a hundred days, Erich gets an unexpected phone call at work. "Mr. Somnolenz? My name is Tobias Prince. I'm a minister and an organizational psychologist. I've heard about your daughter and I believe I may be able to help her. May I come by and see her?"

Erich agrees, and a few hours later Prince sits at the sleeping Venus's side, holding her limp hand in his own and looking deep into her beautiful countenance. "I've seen this before in both businesses and congregations," he tells her parents softly, "though in much a milder form. It's a toxic combination of spiritual apathy and chronic meaninglessness. The good news is, I believe I know the cure."

He leans forward and whispers into Venus's ear, "Listen to me, my sleeping beauty. I can take you away from here—to a life of useful work as well as leisure; to a middle-class condo with only a few selected amenities; to a world of household chores and budget balancing and occasional difficult choices. We won't always have experts to help us or famous people to fawn over us. But we'll make our own decisions and figure things out for ourselves." Then he adds—because, of course, he has fallen deeply in love with her—"We'll take responsibility for our own lives and find our own meaning . . . together."

As he finishes speaking, Venus's eyelids flutter open. She looks deeply into Prince's eyes, smiles, and whispers gently, "Thank God. Take me the hell away from here."

He does, and soon afterward they marry. From then on they live mostly (but not always) happy lives together—not forever after, but to respectably old ages.

Basic Lesson

> **Excluding pertinent individuals from the planning process results in poor outcomes.**

Applications for Serious Managers

When developing an action plan, it can be tempting—and may even seem prudent and logical—to exclude input from people who are considered skeptical or pessimistic. Although this approach is seen as a way to support the process and sidestep sabotage, it might actually cast a pall over the entire process and place the plan on a precipice of inertia to rival Sleeping Beauty's.

Unfortunately, this attitude confuses the planning of a project with its implementation. While no one wants a game plan implemented by doubters, naysayers, and people with little buy-in, the planning phase is a very different story. To plan intelligently, you need a full spectrum of opinions, including those of people who have worries or concerns about the proposed course of action. Indeed, to fully understand the advantages and disadvantages of a tentative plan, it is often essential to ask for—and pay careful attention to—any reasonable objections to it.

The fact is that intelligent challenges can actually help a plan's supporters refine and adjust it and consider problems or risks they might not have anticipated. The more potential problems that are thus anticipated (and, ideally, prepared for) in the planning process, the easier the implementation phase becomes. The more likely it is to succeed as well, because contingencies have been considered and planned for.

Rather than being a barrier to getting a plan or project up and running, critics can serve to actually strengthen it, speed up the process, avoid major pitfalls, and make the end product a better one.

In the worst-case scenario, the concerns of skeptics can be so great, and their voicing of those concerns so convincing, that they prevent moving ahead with the project. In this case, however, isn't that the most appropriate action for the organization as a whole?

A Real-World Business "Tale"

KMS Industries, an electronic equipment manufacturer, was approached by one of its many component vendors, Southwest Circuitry, with a merger proposal. At the time, Southwest supplied expensive microcircuitry for approximately 30 percent of KMS's products. However, the proposal emphasized the capability of the newly merged organization to manufacture more and more of these microcircuit components for its own products; within eight to nine years, the proposal asserted, 100 percent of these components could be manufactured in-house. This opportunity seemed to have incredible bottom-line potential.

At KMS, a seven-member task force was assembled to evaluate whether this potential justified the hefty cash-for-stock exchange necessary to make the deal happen. Duane Petrovsky, the head of New Technology Assessment, was appointed chair of this task force and had full authority to conduct this evaluation. Expense was not an issue, but time certainly was, since the task force had ten days to make a decision.

Duane selected the other six members of his team carefully, balancing engineering types with bean counters. One potential task force member presented an unusual dilemma, however. Marvin Frankel, a senior engineer at KMS, had previously held a similar position at Southwest Circuitry, but he had left for reasons about which he was quite vague. Duane and others at KMS suspected that it had not been an amicable parting of ways, and Duane was concerned that if he included Marvin on the team, he might attempt to undermine the deal as a form of retribution. In the end, Duane decided to play it safe and select a different engineer for the team.

The task force performed admirably, managing to complete the project a day before the deadline and with an assessment that was quite positive. Their five-year projections estimated that fully half the outside manufacturing would be moved internally, and the return on investment showed that the newly merged organization would break even between the third and fourth year. The team concluded that given the current cost of capital and the asking price, the deal made good business sense.

The CEO and CFO of KMS began planning their negotiation strategy. They thoroughly reviewed the task force's voluminous report and polled their board. They also considered what sources of information might have been overlooked. Marvin Frankel's name came up immediately.

The top executives summoned Marvin and summarized for him the task force report, the potential opportunity, the merger plan, and their general negotiation strategy. Then they asked for his opinion—meanwhile assuming that Marvin's bias would result in some highly negative responses.

To their surprise, Marvin had mostly positive things to say about Southwest Circuitry. Although he admitted that he had left the organization amid anger and conflict, the problem, he explained, had been with his superior, not with the company as a whole. Marvin also revealed that quality control had long been a problem at Southwest when handling high volumes of production. (Duane's task force had only asked for general statistics on current production quality.)

Thus the negotiating team was able to add quality control to its list of contractual guarantees. After recalculating their projections so that a lower proportion of component manufacturing would be handled internally, they were able to insist on some downward adjustments to the merger price if these guarantees were not acceptable.

Ultimately, the deal went through, with Southwest accepting the lower price, along with a downstream bonus for reaching specific production and quality targets. The board of directors applauded the negotiating team for its effective strategy, and future annual reports historically reviewed the brilliance of this merger.

With the combining of the two companies' engineering talent and the alignment of incentives for openly collaborating on hitting performance targets, the merged organization met the task force's five-year projections. In addition, Marvin got the computer upgrade he had been requesting for months, as well as an honored position on the CEO's Christmas card list.

The Bottom Line

Avoiding what you do not want to hear does not resolve issues; it just makes you ignorant of them. Tuning out seemingly negative information may seem expedient, especially when you're under the crush of a deadline. Yet if you ignore it, it may reappear in your face later, in a situation you'll wish you had foreseen.

In planning a strategy, rarely is the problem too much information; rather, it is typically too little critical review of the same. If you want to look like a white knight in your own organization, consider as many sources of credible information as possible. This due diligence will not only help you move ahead with confidence, it may also keep you from being blindsided by events you'd failed to consider.

11. THE UGLY DUCKLING

Executive Summary

*A*n obsessive-compulsive mother duck, on maternity leave from routine flock activities, fulfills her interim responsibilities by sitting on her single-parent nest. She remains on this nest until all the eggs hatch—including a tardy, enlarged egg that produces an ungainly, oversize, and seriously ugly duckling.

Though she attempts to teach her entire brood the business of duckhood, soon the barnyard realities become all too clear: Her nonconformist protégé simply is not a good fit with the prevailing corporate culture. For one thing, he is anything but a team player when it comes to most standard duck activities. And as for acquiring the ability to quack, his learning curve is a horizontal line. Worse still, as the ugly duckling grows, his ungainly appearance flouts the familial organization's dress code more each day.

The ugly duckling's siblings ultimately create a hostile environment in which he can no longer thrive or survive. Finally, the duckling is painfully forced to admit that he is at the wrong end of the pecking order. He ceases his activities in the pond in which he was raised and relocates to a marsh where, he hopes, there will be incentives rather than disincentives for someone like him.

Sadly, the move proves unsuccessful. Wild ducks in an adjacent pond quickly squeeze him out of their traditional territory. Loons, which he hopes will be more tolerant of diversity, ultimately maneuver him out of their long-held domain. Although initially welcomed by geese, he quickly discovers that they intend to use him as a distraction for shotgun-wielding hunters. (The geese are quickly shot down, along with their ill-conceived game plan.)

Older and no wiser, this aberrant duck takes refuge on a lake populated by swans. Here, at long last, he finds creatures with the very same demographics, skill sets, and consumption patterns as himself.

In this new organizational setting, his strange appearance and unducklike ways are not only welcomed but familiar. Here he is accepted at last. This awkward duck, whose goose seemed cooked for so long, in the end turns out to be a graceful and able swan.

Basic Lesson

To help your staff members achieve optimal performance, be flexible and tolerant in nurturing their innate skills.

Applications for Serious Managers

The task of all managers is to coordinate the resources at their command to best achieve organizational goals. A major component of those resources is the staff. Finding the right job match for each staff member's unique skill sets may be just as frustrating a search as that of the ugly duckling's.

As most managers know, their job would be a lot simpler were it not for the people they have to manage. Typically, managers believe they are responsible for molding and shaping their staff members into some ideal image of what has worked in the past. In contrast, the most successful managers are able to capitalize on the strengths and weaknesses of each person who reports to them. The best managers channel each person's innate abilities into a useful direction for the organization as a whole. To put it simply, they learn what each person is good at and make sure that the person's job matches her talents.

These two very different approaches, not surprisingly, have quite different results. They also require different mind-sets. In traditional management, each job description is essentially a mold that a staff member is forced into. As necessary, the individual's rough edges are trimmed to comply with the standardized product expected to result. The more flexible approach, however, breaks this mold, reworking each person's duties into a new, nonstandardized iteration of the job description that is (ideally) better or, at the very least, as good as what is created by the traditional one-size-fits-all model.

The managers who are the best at nurturing the innate abilities of their staff members, helping them to blossom into more effective employees, typically do not stop at the boundaries of their areas of responsibility. They may perceive in the skill set of any staff member certain capabilities that are extremely well adapted to some other area of the company. When managers recognize and support these capabilities, they create a triple win: The staff member's career has a better chance of flourishing; the organization gains the most benefit from the employee's enhanced performance; and the manager is more likely to excel within the organization as well.

Sadly, it is the rare organization that is willing to accommodate, much less reward, deviance. Rather, most organizations struggle with an internal contingent of "ugly ducklings" that serve as their own personal albatross. Yet it is those organizations that tolerate new iterations of job descriptions that have the widest range of potential.

In recent years, several large organizations have demonstrated a willingness to be less rigid—and not all of them manufacture outdoor equipment or develop new flavors of espresso. One such organization is Microsoft Corp., which began with a corporate "uniform" defined only by its pocket protector. This was at a time when IBM Corp. owned the computer industry and defined its own culture down to shirt style and tie color. In retrospect, there can be no doubt as to which organization was better positioned to reinvent the future.

Although flexibility is not only tolerated in the arts, but encouraged and expected, the "art of management" is for some reason required to be more regimented. Most corporate palettes might benefit from having more artists with a different eye for organizational color.

A Real-World Business Tale

Deborah Costanzo was the personnel director of a home building supply store that was part of a national chain. Although the store employed a staff of several hundred, Jeff Peebles was the one employee who kept coming back to haunt her. He had rotated through four different departments, but did not seem to fit well with any of his supervisors.

The transfer of Jeff from one department and manager to the next was always rationalized as an attempt to utilize him better. Nevertheless, Deborah suspected that there was an element of dumping the problem from one manager to another. While none of the four managers had anything positive to say about Jeff, the negatives they cited were all relatively minor issues that by themselves were not incriminating and surely not grounds for Jeff's dismissal.

He had started in hardware, but could never seem to completely master the inventory. At the checkout counter he was no master of the keyboard, and he spent a fair amount of time undoing what he had done. In the small-tool area, he demonstrated little aptitude for learning the nuances of the equipment required to promote tools—the most costly items in the store.

While Jeff was pleasant enough and reliable in showing up for work, his apparent lack of motivation frustrated most of the thirty-something-year-old supervisors. As a result, Jeff was a constant topic of discussion at weekly supervisors' meetings.

It was at one of these that Dixon Trumbull, one of Jeff's prior supervisors, noted Jeff's team-building skills when he had organized a store softball team and coordinated a league with other local businesses. As Dixon observed, all of Jeff's prior positions had depended on individual performance and provided for little interaction with his peers.

Based on this observation, the supervisor of logistics, who was responsible for maintaining the inventory and unloading the nightly shipments, suggested that Jeff be transferred to his department. The nightly unpacking, storing, and cataloging of the massive array of items, large and small, required significant coordination among a closely knit crew of workers. It was agreed that the company would try Jeff out in the logistics department for twelve weeks, then reevaluate the situation.

By the end of the following month, it appeared that Jeff had found his niche. Not only did the late-night hours fit his preferred lifestyle of sleeping late into the day, but also he manifested wonderful hand-eye coordination in skillfully manipulating a front-end loader throughout the huge warehouse. In addition, he thrived on the camaraderie of this small band of midnight warriors. He even helped resolve a major problem that had plagued the store since opening day.

The store's residential neighborhood positioned it close to its customers during the day, but at night the loading dock activity—with its bright lights, shouting voices, and beeping loaders—had not endeared the store to its closest neighbors. In fact, those residents had filed frequent complaints with the city council about the lights and noise. Some fines had been levied and paid, but the basic issue remained a sore spot in the community.

When Jeff learned of the problem, he suggested an obvious but previously unconsidered option. If the store relocated the loading dock from the back of the building to the side adjacent to the parking lot, the building itself would provide a buffer for sound and light. As an added benefit, the loaders could maneuver more easily because they could directly access the long main aisles, rather than the short, narrow, cross-connecting lanes. The construction costs were relatively minor, especially since the materials could be budgeted at wholesale cost. Jeff's simple but elegant solution earned him his first-ever year-end bonus.

The Bottom Line

In his best-selling book *The Man Who Listens to Horses*, Monty Roberts describes the different ways to get a horse to accept a saddle. Typically this process is called "breaking the horse" and requires significant force over several weeks. But Roberts finds such an approach objectionable. The spirit that gets crushed in the process, he explains, is the very same one that gives the animal its appeal. This real-time horse whisperer has created a process for "starting" a horse, in which the animal accepts the saddle not out of coercion and force, but because it desires the relationship with the rider that accompanies accepting the saddle.

The process is not only devoid of all force, but it leaves the animal's spirit intact. Also, it only takes about a half-hour.

In management, the ugly duckling approach often breaks the creative spirit of staff members to get them to conform to a rigid model of what has worked in the past. In the process, it lessens their value, because their willingness to take a risk and ability to think outside the box have been squelched. So has their uniqueness.

More problematic still are the staff members with enough fortitude to refuse to be broken—the ones who never seem to fit into the organization. They drift from department to department until they either leave of their own volition or finally commit some offense that merits dismissal. Yet that fortitude, when appropriately channeled, could significantly benefit your organization—or, in some cases, even revolutionize it. Sadly, in most cases, such people usually end up working for a more tolerant competitor.

The next time someone on your staff starts to look ugly, consider trying to find the grace and beauty beneath it all. If you cannot, then consider who in your organization may be able to capitalize on what you see only as a downside.

12. THE HARE AND THE TORTOISE

Executive Summary

hare is well known throughout the forest for the speed with which he does business. He has a reputation for using all the latest technology to make an endless string of deals in nest construction, burrow digging, stream damming, egg hatching, and so on.

The hare has a cellular phone, a laptop, a pager, state-of-the-art e-mail, and an all-in-one fax machine, scanner, printer, and carrot slicer. The hare is always busy, always moving, and always making promises—but he never seems quite focused enough to follow through on his promises.

The tortoise, on the other hand, seems slow. She does business the old-fashioned way, working hard and staying extremely focused. She has few high tech toys, yet she always manages to return other animals' calls promptly, and she completes every project she takes on. In fact, the tortoise is the only animal in the whole forest who says "no" to work she doesn't think she can complete.

One summer the hare and the tortoise both decide to run for the position of governor of the forest. Soon they become fierce political competitors. Not surprisingly, the hare runs a glitzy, high tech, and highly negative campaign, constantly putting down the tortoise for her slowness and "backward" ways of doing things. The tortoise, on the other hand, ignores the hare's attacks and simply speaks to the issues in speeches that are focused, steady, and well thought out, if somewhat slow in their delivery.

As election day nears, the two candidates decide to have a public race to see which one is truly the most efficient and productive. The tortoise's handlers try to convince her to change her mind, but she just says, "Don't worry. I know the hare and I'm almost sure I can win."

On the day of the big race, all the animals in the forest come out to watch the event. The hare shows up wearing top-of-the-line Nikes, an expensive running suit, his pager, cellular phone, laptop, a portable fax machine, and a Walkrabbit with a CD called "Affirmations for Speed." The tortoise wears nothing but her usual shell. The two candidates shake paws and take their places at the starting line. The owl counts them down: "Ready, set, compete!" The two animals take off.

Almost immediately, the hare takes a substantial lead. As he reaches the middle of the course, however, his pager goes off. He is so far ahead of the tortoise that he decides to take out his cell phone and return the call. But there are too many trees in the way for his cell phone to work, so he decides to hop over to a clearing and make his call.

As soon as he gets to the clearing, another call comes in. The hare takes it, then returns the page. Then he decides to check his e-mail. Then he receives several faxes and has to return several more calls. Soon he gets so busy making deals that he forgets about the tortoise and the race.

Meanwhile, the tortoise stays focused and puts 100 percent of her effort into reaching the finish line. She does nothing but move her chubby little legs, one in front of the other, as fast as she can.

Midway through the course, she spots the hare in a distant clearing. His back is to her and he is nodding vigorously, holding his cell phone close to his long, floppy ear. The tortoise just smiles, returns her attention to the race, and keeps walking.

An hour later, the hare finishes typing his notes from his last call, pleased at the new deals he has made. He snaps shut his laptop, looks up, and with a shock suddenly realizes where he is and how distracted he has become. In a panic, he leaves all of his communication devices there in the clearing and begins hopping as fast as he can toward the end of the course. But as he makes the last turn, he sees the tortoise cross the finish line, ten hops ahead of him.

Publicly humiliated, the hare drops out of the governor's race. The tortoise, on the other hand, serves as governor of the forest for several years and later accepts a lucrative endorsement deal from a leading walking shoe manufacturer.

Basic Lesson

> To be successful, an organization needs to have a clear focus.

Applications for Serious Managers

New companies usually start out highly focused on a single product or service, and that focus is usually codified in a mission statement. The company knows exactly where it is and where it is going. It creates and delivers a specific product or service with clearly defined objectives and goals. Just as the tortoise did, the young, focused company works hard to achieve its goals, one step at a time.

However, as companies mature, their focus tends to broaden and they typically begin a process of diversification—often because they have accumulated cash reserves and can afford to buy up other companies. But this diversification is not always wise. In fact, losing focus of your primary objective usually results in failure. Some examples: In the 1980s, IBM Corp. bought Rolm, Coca-Cola bought Columbia Pictures, and Eastman Kodak bought Sterling Drug. Yet all three of these signature companies sold these purchases at a loss before six years had passed.

A company that has established a brand name may feel it can carry that name into other industries and successfully carry out a process of line extension. Yet unless a new industry, product, or service is a natural fit, the principle of line extension may prove foolhardy. After all, would you buy Adidas cologne just because you own a pair of Adidas running shoes? Would you try LifeSavers frozen vegetables just because you already purchase LifeSavers candy? Consider this sobering thought: Most new products in the United States are line extensions, yet only 10 percent of such products are successful enough to still be marketed after two years.

Companies often lose focus by investing their capital and management talents in entirely new areas that they think (translation: guess, hope, wish, or pray) may be profitable. Yet companies that divert their energies and resources into a variety of products often find that the new products never catch on. Meanwhile, partly due to in-house neglect, the profits of their original product diminish as well.

A Real-World Business "Tale"

Marjorie Spano and her daughter Susan had worked in the design industry for many years. Their dream was to design and market their own line of clothing and see their creations in upscale department and specialty stores across the nation.

To accomplish their dream, they created a business plan and obtained significant capital from venture capitalists. Their designs were aimed at mature, professional women who had the money to spend $300 to $500 for a jacket and $150 to $250 for a matching skirt.

Marjorie and Susan were quite clever in their sizing practices. Although their clothing was sized X-small, small, medium, large, and X-large, someone who wore a size 10–12 could fit into their size small. Soon the Spano line built up an excellent following. Dedicated customers waited patiently for their new seasonal designs, and every year their clothing became more and more popular.

Marjorie and Susan decided to use the Spano name on more products. They reasoned that if well-to-do professional women wanted Spano suits, then surely the middle-of-the-road working woman would be delighted by the chance to buy some less expensive outfits with the Spano label. For this market, they created suits that cost $150 to $200 for the skirt and jacket together. They also launched lines of handbags, jewelry, and perfume, hoping for a large, fast upward jump in sales and profits. The venture capitalists smelled a hot thing and were only too eager to put up the money for all of these new products.

But all too quickly things started going sour. Susan and Marjorie, who had previously focused much of their attention on their favorite part of the business, product design, now were forced to spend sixty to seventy hours a week just running the company. They quickly discovered they had too many products to design and not enough time to do it in. Soon they found it impossible to maintain the quality that their dedicated, professional clientele demanded. Eventually they hired professional designers and, with great regret, turned their full attention to being corporate executives.

For the first time, Marjorie and Susan began to disagree and argue, often about trivia. Their relationship grew more and more strained. Eighteen months after the big expansion, both of them dreaded going to work, where they barely spoke to each other. After two years, Spano Corporation declared Chapter 11 bankruptcy, abandoned all its spin-off lines and products, and went back to its main focus: business clothes for the mature professional woman. Fortunately, it made the switch in time and the company survived—as did the relationship between mother and daughter.

The Bottom Line

A successful business must take a lesson from the tortoise: Stay focused and keep an eye on the target at all times. Slow, steady, and focused usually proves to be the winning strategy, rather than uncontrolled growth at any cost.

13. PUSS IN BOOTS

Executive Summary

 miller, nearing retirement, decides to divest himself of all his holdings. In the hope of avoiding probate court, as well as any potential tax consequences, he transfers ownership of all his assets to his three sons. The eldest son gets the mill, the second son gets the family donkey, and the youngest son inherits the S corporation's pussycat.

The youngest son bemoans his fate and his poverty, for the market value of the cat is far below that of either the mill or the donkey. Indeed, the only way he can envision that the cat will add value is to cook it up as a tough but somewhat nourishing supper.

The cat, however, has a suggestion for his new master. "I have more on my mind than just napping in the sun," he says. "In fact, I have some ideas for a joint venture. I'll invest the sweat equity, but you will have to capitalize this organization with a pair of good leather boots and a stout sack with a drawstring." The son is intrigued, so the appropriate legal documents are drafted and signed and the partnership officially consummated.

The cat, wearing his new leather boots to better withstand the rigors of life on the road, sets out with his sack and a box of business cards. His card reads, "Puss in Boots, Senior Executive Vice President of Corporate Development."

Over the next few days, Puss in Boots traps a number of rabbits and several partridges in the sack. He then travels to the nearby capital and presents them to the elderly king as "a gift of admiration from my superior, the CEO of Carabas, Inc." The king graciously accepts the gifts, but is as bewildered as everyone else by a cat that talks, walks on two legs, has a boot fetish, and lugs around a bag full of small game.

Later that week, as the king tours his kingdom with his beautiful daughter (conveniently named Princess), he encounters the magical cat once again. This time, however, the cat is in serious distress. "Help!" he screams. "Our company has been set upon by corporate raiders! They acquired a controlling interest through a leveraged buyout. My superior, the CEO of Carabas, was given thirty minutes to clean out his desk and vacate the premises. Then the new owners took his clothes and threw him in the swimming pool to drown!"

The king, eager to repay the CEO's earlier kindness—and hoping to learn more about this fast-talking, well-shod cat—sends his security people to rescue the miller's son, who they find doing laps in the neighborhood pool. The king's minions coax him out, outfit him in royal garments, and bring him before the king and his daughter.

Princess gets a good look at the miller's son—dressed to the teeth in royal vestments and well muscled from his years of hard work in the mill—and falls immediately and incurably in love with him. As for the miller's son, he is smitten just as quickly by Princess's eyes, smile, hair, body, royal blood, family connections, financial holdings, rights of inheritance, and absolute power. Of course, this is exactly what Puss in Boots has in mind. He rubs gently against Princess's legs, purring and whispering under his breath, "Okay, royal family, it's miller time."

Puss in Boots then suggests to the love-struck duo that they visit his master's home, which Puss in Boots describes as exquisite and palatial, but which is in fact a small basement one-bedroom flat. The conniving cat rushes on ahead and—using his quick tongue, his feline wiles, and people's inherent willingness to take orders from highly assertive creatures wearing expensive footwear—convinces everyone in the building to pretend to recognize the miller's son as their landlord. (This isn't terribly difficult, since a faceless management firm owns the high-rise.) The huge building and her beau's ostensible ownership of it deeply impress Princess, who—not to put too fine a point on it—has a thing for wealth and power.

The cat in the Doc Martens then takes the elevator to the penthouse, which is owned by a Hong Kong billionaire who uses it only a few weeks a year. Puss in Boots picks the lock with his claws and ushers the happy couple inside the empty apartment.

The rest is history. Puss in Boots gets rid of the building's super—a lazy, incompetent, ogrelike man—by using his powers of persuasion to get the fellow a better-paying job as an intern for Jerry Springer. And soon thereafter, Princess and the miller's son are wed.

Thus, in a very short time, this newly organized joint venture is able to pay off all outstanding debt on the boots and sack, while the miller's son is in line to inherit the entire kingdom when the aged king dies. In the end, everyone lives happily ever after—except for Jerry Springer, who is soon run out of the kingdom by angry peasants.

Basic Lesson

> **Take control of circumstances or they will take control of you.**

Applications for Serious Managers

Nothing fits the managerial stereotype more than aggressive action. In reality, though, actually doing something proactive may be expecting too much from most managers. (Sadly, the great majority of managers tend to prefer more familiar corporate games such as dodge the bullet, generate a memo, and pass the buck.)

Managers must cultivate a variety of skills in order to become adept at functioning proactively. First of all, they must become aware of the limitations of their personal perspective, which is a complex product of their training, experience, culture, gender, religion, politics, ethnicity, and other factors. Once they are aware that their perspective is only one interpretation of reality, they can start collecting some others. Initially, the miller's son could only see his new cat's potential in the narrow perspective of a potential meal. The cat, however, had a very different vision of the future.

A second invaluable skill in being more proactive is the ability to identify emerging trends. While some people naturally have this ability, it can also be learned simply by closely observing the patterns that develop around us. An early sensitivity to these patterns, and the ability to extrapolate their future growth or direction, equals proactivity.

A third key to proactivity is the ability to shrug off the myths, rituals, stereotypes, and beliefs that frame—and thus limit—the options we consider. (Puss in Boots was not limited by sentimental images of cute, helpless cats napping lazily in the sun. Instead, he created an entirely new image for himself, complete with boots, while envisioning and carrying out a complex scenario that no one else could have predicted.)

A final characteristic conducive to proactivity is a high level of energy. While some of us no doubt have a genetic proclivity toward working faster, longer, and harder, we place our money on the people who work smarter. Specifically, we suggest identifying those things that you are already doing well enough and not expending any more energy on them.

This may seem counterintuitive at first. Our natural inclination is to continue to do a lot of what we already do well, because it is comfortable and rewarding. But we say, get over it! You may have noticed that our feline hero gave up his regular job of mousing in the mill to take on his new, self-determined responsibilities. If he had tried to do both, he probably would not have been effective at either one.

Our Puss in Boots was an archetype of proactivity.

A Real-World Business "Tale"

Roger Moressy and Calvin Ross started RossMore Bikes over a decade ago. Both men were engineers who met when they were employees for a national bicycle manufacturer. After a year of planning, they started their own regional brand of low-cost bikes distributed through large discount stores. Their niche marketing approach was successful and they had little competition from the major manufacturers, who distributed primarily through specialty bicycle stores. They focused their efforts on refining the manufacturing process and making shrewd purchases of materials to maintain their price edge while still delivering a quality bike.

Cal was backpacking in California when he first noticed a group of aging hippies coasting down the mountainsides on old Schwinn beach cruisers. Dismissing them at first, he nonetheless noted their reinforced frames and heavy-duty shocks.

Cal's son was heavily into dirt bike racing, and some years earlier, RossMore had developed some BMX models for its own market—knobby tires, shock absorbers, and all. It turned out to be a moderately successful line. Although racing bikes were also soaring in popularity, Cal and Roger had ignored that trend because racing-bike customers were not price sensitive, but focused instead on quality, weight, and gear mechanisms. Still, something about the two trends gnawed at the partners.

It was finally Roger who pulled it all together. "Mountain bikes," he said. "That's our new line." Mountain bikes were beginning to appear on the West Coast, but the major manufacturers had all ignored this trend and all current lines were being produced by boutique companies. While this was an upscale market, similar to the market for racing bikes, mountain bikes were a purely American phenomenon, with virtually no European or Asian competition.

Roger and Cal's dirt bike expertise gave them an inroad into some of the required technology and supplies needed to produce mountain bikes, but marketing was a different challenge, since this was not a product for their current customers.

Roger focused on the design and manufacturing aspects while Cal did procurement and marketing. Nine months later, RossMore began cranking out an impressive line of pricey, rugged, all-terrain bikes that were distributed through specialty stores. Their customers were demanding, but they were willing to pay for high quality. The creative challenge turned out to be a welcome revitalization of the two men's engineering skills, and within two years RossMore's RockMore line represented 32 percent of the company's volume, 69 percent of its revenue, and more than 80 percent of its margin. Meanwhile, all the major manufacturers were struggling with shrinking market share as their customers shifted to product lines that were only available from specialty manufacturers.

The Bottom Line

Obviously, we need to be proactive about becoming proactive. While proactivity is a quality almost universally desired and revered in CEOs, in reality it needs to be integrated into all levels of management. The more widespread proactivity becomes in your own organization, the more energy the organization has to change from what it has become into what it truly needs to be.

The skills necessary to support proactivity can be taught, acquired, practiced, and strengthened. Knowing the limits of your perspective (and paying attention to others'), identifying trends, envisioning potential options, and working smart are useful skills for anyone to have. We strongly recommend nurturing their development, rewarding their use, and encouraging their application—not only in others, but also in yourself.

In other words, grab your boots, plus a stout sack, and hit the road.

14. THE STEADFAST TIN SOLDIER

Executive Summary

wenty-five soldiers, all cast from the same spoonful of tin, regularly fulfill their mission of pleasing and amusing a small boy. Their job descriptions require them to stand at attention in the playroom until the boy is ready to play with them, at which point they are expected to remain standing while he lines them up, moves them around, throws them at each other, and occasionally buries them in his sandbox.

One of the soldiers is lacking a leg. This is no problem for the boy, who is an equal opportunity employer and recognizes that the one-legged soldier is well qualified for the position of Durable and Immobile Toy despite his handicap. However, the one-legged soldier does lack self-esteem—which, frankly, is not our problem, inasmuch as he has not bothered to consult with either the tin staff psychiatrist or the tin chaplain.

On the other side of the room stands a beautiful cardboard ballerina whose duties also involve remaining rigid and unmoving. From the tin soldier's viewpoint, she too seems to be missing a leg, although in fact it is merely raised behind her. ("It's like the glass ceiling for women in the child amusement field," the ballerina often tells herself. "You can't see it, but you know it's there.")

As the two toys—one of tin, one of cardboard—stare at each other day after day, they start to fall in love. The tin soldier dreams of someday receiving his honorable discharge, beginning a new career as an ADA compliance consultant, marrying the ballerina, and living happily ever after with her in their own little corner of the playroom.

Nevertheless, despite their constant eye contact, the two never speak a word to one another or move from their frozen positions—not even between midnight and dawn, when all the other playroom toys go off duty. During these hours, the other soldiers play cards, polish their tin rifles, and occasionally hit on the ballerina. But the ballerina (who's basically a serious workaholic) ignores them, remains in position, and continues staring into the adoring eyes of the one-legged soldier, who simply cannot bring himself to act outside of his clearly delineated duties.

One day the tin soldier falls from the playroom window into the street below. Predictably, he responds with his traditional workplace strategy of standing still and staring straight ahead. Then rain pours down and street urchins sail him down the gutter in a paper boat, but the tin soldier merely holds his rifle tighter and soldiers on, repeating his company's mission statement to himself.

Eventually the boat plunges into the ocean and disintegrates while a fish swallows our hero. *I don't know what to do*, he thinks. *My twenty-four brothers and I were removed from our cardboard box long ago, but I still don't know how to think outside the box. All I know how to do is clutch my rifle and stay immobile.*

Eventually the fish is caught and sold to the household cook, who discovers the tin soldier when she guts the fish. Miraculously, she returns him to the very same playroom. But our rigid hero still has not learned to develop his emotional competence in the workplace. So, with longing in their hearts, the tin soldier and cardboard ballerina go back to their daily grind of staring at each other unflinchingly. (Can you imagine trying to calculate the opportunity cost on this pathetic relationship?)

One evening, an unexpected reorganization of playroom personnel occurs when a gust of wind blows both the soldier and the ballerina into the roaring fire in the fireplace. In less than a minute, the ballerina is gone forever and by the next morning, all that remains of the solider is a heart-shaped lump of tin.

Unable to adapt to new situations or make proactive decisions, in the end the tin soldier is forced by circumstances to abandon his career and take a considerably less skilled position as a heart-shaped paperweight.

Basic Lesson

> **If you fail to function proactively, you'd better prepare to accept the consequences.**

Applications for Serious Managers

It is not by coincidence that this fairy tale follows "Puss in Boots," for the two are companion pieces. If "Puss in Boots" is the truth, then "The Steadfast Tin Soldier" is the consequence, for we see in this tale the typical result of being reactive rather than proactive.

Ultimately, "The Steadfast Tin Soldier" is not a poignant little tale of unrequited love as much as it is a tragedy of lost opportunity. This fairy tale expresses the results of both reactivity and inflexibility in a stark and emotionally engaging way that few case studies can duplicate.

Nevertheless, this is a particularly apt parable for our times. Everything in it hinges on that description of being "steadfast." Is that wording an appreciation of the tin soldier's reliability and constancy or a pejorative reference to his head-in-the-sand, grin-and-bear-it stoicism? Do you want your own staff to soldier on and roll with the punches or take the bull by the horns and make a difference? Choose your analogy.

What could our tragic hero have done differently? Just about anything would have been an improvement. First of all, he could have taken advantage of that classic midnight reprieve and gotten acquainted with the ballerina. Second, if he had analyzed the obvious patterns, he would have realized that he was in a high-risk occupation and she might not have been willing to accept that. Third, had he looked at the situation honestly, he might have questioned how durable a match could be made between a tarnish-resistant career soldier and a cardboard performance artist lacking in dimension. Ultimately, he might have concluded that their relationship would have crashed and burned anyway.

We find it hard to feel sorry for such a passive character, particularly one who has supposedly been victimized by circumstances that, in all fairness, were only partly beyond his control. While perhaps we can tolerate such behavior in a fairy tale, personally and professionally it is not a behavioral model with much career potential.

A Real-World Business "Tale"

Although an abstract case study might not rival the dramatic consequences portrayed by the tin soldier, truth is often stranger than fiction. Thus, the serious downside of being reactive to the marketplace, rather than proactive, is effectively demonstrated in *Big Blues: The Unmaking of IBM* (Crown, 1994) by Paul Carroll of *The Wall Street Journal*. This engaging, reality-based tale summarizes the decline of IBM Corp. in the late 1980s and early 1990s, detailing the capitulation of its leadership position in the computing industry to Microsoft as a consequence of IBM's failing to recognize the handwriting on the information technology wall until it was too late.

Entering the decade of the 1980s, IBM was struggling with its development of the personal computer. IBM owned the mainframe market and had gradually surpassed the earlier leads of General Electric, Burroughs, Univac, NCR, Control Data, and Honeywell. Seizing the lead on PC development away from Xerox at the beginning of the decade, it failed to assume a leadership role in spite of internal projections of the crippling impact impending market changes would have on IBM's business.

Spawned in a marketplace that evolved from computers large enough to fill a building, the concept of the PC was never a very comfortable one at IBM, which still referred to the PC as a "home computer." After all, IBM had fulfilled the 1949 prediction of *Popular Mechanics* that "computers in the future may perhaps only weigh 1.5 tons." As the leader in producing such machines for business, IBM was much more likely to buy into the philosophy of Kenneth Olsen, the president and founder of Digital Equipment Corporation, who in 1977 said, "There is no reason for any individual to have a computer in their home."

Most of IBM's managers remained oblivious to the changes going on in the marketplace around them, feeling instead that the only competition in the computing industry was internally among themselves. It was said that the sun never set on IBM because its success overseas against foreign rivals such as Olivetti, Bull, and ICL was as stunning as its dominance in the U.S. marketplace. Although IBM's marginal interest in the PC (in combination with its substantial organizational momentum) allowed it to displace pioneering Tandy and upstart Kaypro, IBM was also fortunate that Apple Computer, whose entire identity focused on the PC, was so effective at hamstringing itself.

Like the tin soldier gazing longingly at the ballerina, IBM engaged in wishful thinking about the potential of PCs, but its actions never fulfilled its intent. IBM produced several half-baked PC attempts in the SCAMP, Datamaster, and 5100 series, then entertained an option to buy computers from Atari and anoint them with the IBM logo. In fact, the product design team established in 1980 to rectify this status developed its budget and presentation on bootlegged Apple computers, in spite of having access to unlimited amounts of IBM hardware.

Adding the ultimate insult of ignoring the potential for PC software to the very serious injury of PC hardware impotence, IBM gradually sealed its fate. At a time when IBM employed a staff of 340,000 with $27 billion in assets, $26 billion in sales, and $3.6 billion in profits, it turned to the thirty-two computer geeks at Microsoft to develop software to run on the IBM PC. When an operating system was required to handle that software, Bill Gates directed IBM to a homegrown version, QDOS (which stood for "quick and dirty operating system"), developed by programmers in Seattle. Gates arranged for the rights to be purchased for $75,000, but IBM wanted nothing to do with it. So Microsoft acquired the rights to what would eventually become the disk operating system (DOS) and started down the road to displace IBM's preeminence.

While IBM has regained much of its past luster in the late 1990s, it may never again see the heady levels of success it had attained very early on. Trapped between the rock of failed PC development and the hard place of a shrinking mainframe market, IBM lost $75 billion of stock-market value, or more than the total worth of the next largest company. At the zenith of its success, the worth of IBM exceeded that of all the publicly held companies in Germany, while at the nadir of its despair, IBM wrote off $20 billion in assets. In spite of its seemingly unsurpassable status in the computer industry, IBM was severely punished by the marketplace for failing to use that status proactively and for reacting only when necessary.

The Bottom Line

Taking action always carries a certain risk—but so does limiting your response to fixing the outcomes of the problem rather than the problem itself.

Proactivity, flexibility, and innovation are three of the best tools any manager can wield. Like any tool, each of these practices can be used wisely or badly. When used wisely, they can transform your company. But even when used only marginally well, they can still yield better outcomes than rigidity, inaction, and stuck-in-the-box thinking.

Let us not forget that doing nothing is still doing something—it's just not the most appropriate thing. Since every action (including inaction) yields some consequences, reactivity and inflexibility will have their own results.

If that is the route you choose, however, the only unknown is whether those results become your personal frying pan, the last stop on the way to the fire. And when eventually the smoke clears, no one will particularly care what residue you left behind in the ashes.

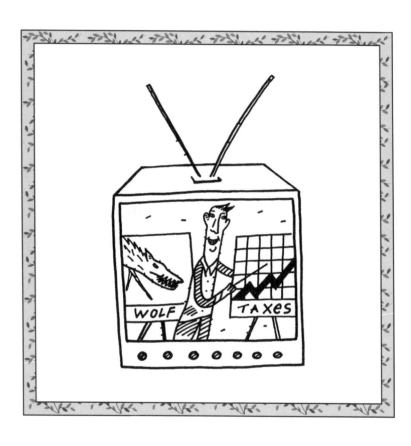

15. THE BOY WHO CRIED WOLF

Executive Summary

After meeting with his accountant, a young, well-to-do sheep rancher discovers that in the previous year his ranch lost money for the first time. "It's a combination of depressed wool prices, increased taxes on your land, and the cost of that new truck you're driving," the accountant explains.

"Well, what can I do about it?" the rancher wants to know.

"You can sell the ranch. Or you can sell the truck. Or you can pray that prices rise. Take your pick."

"Would media attention help?" the rancher wonders.

"It seems to work for Madonna. Probably couldn't hurt you any, either."

The rancher thinks the situation over, then drives across town to the local television station. Inside, he finds a reporter and tells her, "A wolf killed two of my sheep last night. I wouldn't have believed it if I hadn't watched it happen myself."

The reporter perks up immediately. "A wolf?" she says. "There hasn't been a sighting of a wolf in this county since 1968."

"So is this worth a story?"

"You bet. I'll bring a crew out to your place later this afternoon."

A few hours later the TV crew arrives. They are particularly interested in filming the two sheep carcasses, but the rancher explains, "I don't think I could easily find the spot. I have eleven thousand acres, you know. But I saw that wolf just as plain as day, tearing the belly right out of each of those sheep. And I tell you, that's exactly what the whole ranching industry is doing to people like me, tearing out our bellies. What we need is stronger price supports for wool, and we need them now. When is our government finally going to stick up for working people like us ranchers?"

The piece airs on the evening news, and the next day the rancher finds that he has become a minor celebrity in town. His fellow ranchers are particularly pleased with his comments on price supports.

Two weeks later, when the rancher returns from a vacation, he gets bad news from one of his ranch hands: Poachers have stolen at least two dozen of his sheep.

"Well, hell. Think we can get the TV people to cover it?"

"This isn't Jesse James and the great train robbery. It's common poaching. There's nothing to cover."

"That's where you're wrong," the rancher says. "Watch the news tomorrow night."

The next day the rancher calls up the television station and asks for the same reporter. "This time I've got a whole slew of sheep missing," he insists. "And it wasn't just one wolf this time, but a whole pack. I saw them come slinking down out of the hills like hyenas. There must have been eight or nine of them."

"We'll be right down," the reporter says.

This time the rancher leads the crew to a spot in the middle of his land. "It was around here somewhere," he says. "I remember, because the wolves came down from those hills over there." The reporter and her cameraman both seem skeptical of the story—especially when, in the middle of the interview, the rancher suddenly changes the topic from wolves to the general plight of ranchers and the lack of government support for the ranching industry. Still, a short piece airs on the local news that night, making the rancher a temporary celebrity in town once again.

A few days later the rancher gets more bad news from one of his ranch hands: "We've got an anthrax problem. Ten of your sheep are dead already. There's no telling how many more have been infected."

Furious, the rancher picks up the phone and calls his accountant. "Why am I in this business anyway?" he asks. "If I wanted to lose money like this, I could just go to Las Vegas and gamble it away. It'd be a whole lot quicker and easier."

"Las Vegas is a fourteen-hour drive," his accountant reminds him. "But with sheep, you don't have to leave your house to lose money efficiently."

"Thanks for the encouragement," the rancher says and hangs up.

He calls the TV station again and asks for the reporter. When she comes on the line, he says, "You won't believe this, but last night I saw no less than twenty wolves on my property. . . ."

The reporter hangs up on him.

A month passes. No other sheep have come down with anthrax, and for a while things are pretty much back to normal for the rancher's business. Then, one morning, one of his ranch hands bursts into his office, looking pale and upset. "What's up?" the rancher asks.

"Get in your truck with me," the man says grimly. "I have something to show you." The two men drive out to the far edge of the rancher's land, close to the foothills of the Rockies. There, amid the stones and scrub, lie two mutilated, partially eaten sheep carcasses. "There's only one explanation for this," the ranch hand says. "Wolves have returned to the county, just like you've been saying on TV. I think we need to let people know about this."

The rancher looks off into the distance, then shakes his head slowly. "Don't see much point in it," he says sadly. "No one's going to believe a word I say now."

Basic Lesson

> **Do not squander your political capital.**

Applications for Serious Managers

Although you won't read about political capital in any management textbook, it is a very real and necessary phenomenon in business. The rancher cried wolf needlessly and did not understand the problem of wasting political capital; don't make the same mistake!

Political capital consists of favors and attention that are owed to you, or that you are entitled to receive for some other reason. In business, it is a currency that may be worth far more to you than cash.

Political capital is earned when you go beyond the general expectations of your job—by volunteering to stay late and finish a project, taking on additional projects, writing a reference for a friend's child, or using your connections to help someone get a job. Although political capital is rarely discussed, most of us understand how it is accrued, tracked, and used.

With few exceptions, one's political capital is quite limited and thus should be used only when absolutely needed. Just as you should borrow your best money last, you should spend your political capital only when no other form of currency will do.

Unfortunately, many naive businesspeople use up their political capital when other forms of currency may be more appropriate, on the erroneous assumption that more of it can be generated as easily as investment capital.

A good deal of political capital is usually available to people when they first begin a new job, career, or business. Sometimes this is called a "honeymoon" period, where people will happily assist you or overlook mistakes because you are new. However, although you may not be aware of it at the time, you are using up political capital that you may not yet have accumulated. As a result, you owe people. And you will be asked and expected to pay; it's just a matter of time.

We must emphasize here that any payback you provide must follow ethical business practices. The moral standards that apply to political capital are no different from those that apply to other business dealings. If you are asked for a favor that requires you to go outside the law, violate your (or your company's) principles, or risk getting yourself (or someone else) into trouble, the only appropriate response is, "I'm sorry, but I can't."

Although people normally keep careful track of who owes them what and what they owe others, the exchange of political capital is normally not discussed. Any overt discussion of the subject is usually frowned upon, and it is considered extremely bad form to say to someone, "You owe me." Most people understand when you are paying back a favor, or when you are accumulating some political capital by doing one for them.

Remember that political capital is not only related to the efforts you expend, but to your position in (and history with) your company. Some people are able to give more than others. Therefore, never feel that you owe more than you are able to give—and don't ask others to give more than they can. If you promise or ask for the impossible, you are setting yourself up for failure and disappointment.

Our overall advice: Accumulate political capital whenever possible, spend it sparingly, and always keep plenty of it banked. You never know when you may need to make a large (and perhaps unexpected) withdrawal.

A Real-World Business "Tale"

Andrew Goldman was an M.D. in a four-physician clinic. A devoted family man, Andrew made a point of spending his weekends with his wife and children whenever possible, taking them to the beach, on ski outings, and on quick trips to nearby cities and attractions.

Although he was on call every fourth weekend, Andrew frequently asked one of his colleagues—all of whom were single—to cover for him. "My kids are really counting on this trip," he would explain, or "This is the only weekend all five of us could get reservations."

Andrew's colleagues were very accommodating for the first two years that he was with the clinic, but eventually his regular requests began to get on their nerves. It seemed as if every other time he was going to be on call, he would be asking for someone to fill in for him. As Kyoko Katagiri, one of the other physicians, put it to her fiancé, "He thinks that because we're single, we don't have lives or obligations of our own on weekends."

Kyoko even raised the issue directly with Andrew, but to her surprise he just brushed it off. "Wait till you have kids of your own," he said. "Then you'll understand how important it is to spend time with them, especially when you have three—four, once the new baby arrives."

Frustrated, the other three physicians met to discuss the matter. They made an agreement that for the next year, none of them would take over for Andrew on weekends unless he became ill or disabled.

Two weeks afterward, late on a Friday afternoon, Andrew got an unexpected call from his wife. "Honey, I know it is six weeks early, but my water just broke and I'm having contractions. I'm packing up right now to go to the hospital."

Anxiously, Andrew relayed the news to Kyoko, who would be delivering the baby. He finished with his last patient of the day and started to pack up. Then, with a shock, Andrew realized that he was on call for the weekend, starting in ten minutes.

He asked both of the other physicians to cover for him, but each of them said, "I'm sorry Andy, but I've already made plans."

Nearly frantic, Andrew pleaded, "Can't you change those plans?" But both of his colleagues said that although they were very sorry, they couldn't.

Andrew rushed to join his wife at the hospital, where they spent the next two hours together. But then Andrew's beeper went off and he had to attend to a patient at another hospital across town. As a result, he missed witnessing the birth of his second daughter—something he and his wife both regretted for many years to come.

The Bottom Line

Accumulate political capital whenever you reasonably can, but spend it judiciously and only on truly important things. Squandering your political capital on conveniences and petty desires will leave you high and dry at precisely those times when you need it the most.

16. CHICKEN LITTLE

Executive Summary

hicken Little is lounging outside the henhouse, reading *The Wall Street Journal* on a hot, lazy afternoon. Chicken Little follows the market closely, for she has a substantial, nicely diversified portfolio as well as a strong interest in commodities, particularly corn.

Soon Chicken Little falls asleep, rolls onto her back, and begins daydreaming about her wealth, snoring as only a chicken can. In her dream, she decides to go long on soybean meal.

Then an acorn falls out of a tree and strikes her on the head. Chicken Little awakens with a start, convinced that something is terribly amiss. She rubs her head, stares up at the sky, and quickly puts two and two together.

"Oh, my goodness!" she exclaims. "Sky is falling!"

Chicken Little quickly checks her portfolio to see how many shares of sky she owns. It is quite a bit—so much, in fact, that it frightens her. *If sky is falling,* she thinks, *I must sell all my shares before it drops even further. I'm going to tell my broker immediately.* So Chicken Little starts out for the Smith Barney office to tell her broker to sell sky.

But before she gets very far, Chicken Little meets Henny Penny, her cousin. "Sky is falling," she tells Henny Penny nervously. "Mark my words, we are headed for a huge bear market—for sky, for clouds, for everything in between outer space and the ground. I'm dumping all of my sky before it hits bottom."

123

Henny Penny gasps. "I always thought of sky as a blue-chip investment."

"Do what you want," Chicken Little replies, "but I'm getting out. Are you coming with me or not?"

Henny Penny thinks for a moment. "I'm coming!" she says hastily. She packs a bag with some grain and the current *Investor's Business Daily*, and together the pair continues on in the direction of their broker's office.

A little farther up the road they see Cocky Locky, who is busy eating grubs and reading stock quotations on his laptop. "Where are the two of you headed in such a hurry?" Cocky asks.

Chicken Little replies, "We're going to see our broker. Have you heard? Sky is taking a nosedive."

Cocky tilts her head back and forth. "You know, I think I remember Faith Popcorn saying something about sky. Do you really think it's time to get out?"

Now Chicken Little is sure that sky is plummeting, because she has a deep and abiding trust in anyone who has "corn" in their name. "Do I think it's time to get out?" she nearly shrieks. "If we don't get out now, we'll lose our feathers!" This convinces Cocky, who quickly joins the first two on their journey.

As they get closer to their broker's office, the group runs into Goosey Loosey and then Ducky Lucky. Both of them listen to Chicken Little's tale and decide to join the other birds on their pilgrimage.

They are almost at their broker's office when Foxy Woxy appears out of an alley. He smiles at the group. "What's up?" he asks. "You look like five fowl on a mission."

Chicken Little says firmly, "We're on our way to our broker. We need to get rid of all our sky. Haven't you heard? It's about to crash and burn."

Foxy Woxy's smile grows broader. "I see. And just what kind of commission is your broker getting?" He reaches into his fur, pulls out a stack of business cards, and passes them out. "I ask because I run a discount brokerage. At Woxycorp, we can do all your trading for one-third the commission of traditional brokers. Not only that, but I've got a convenient office location, right here in my den. Why don't the five of you step inside and see how I can help?"

The birds all look at each other. "Sounds good to me," says Chicken Little, always on the lookout for a bargain. "Come on, let's try it." And they all follow Foxy Woxy into his den.

Foxy Woxy closes the door firmly behind them. "Well, now," he says softly, "let's see how I can help. In fact, let's see how I can help myself to supper!" And with that, he pounces on the five fowl one after another, rips open their throats, and devours them one by one.

On that day, the sky really does fall for all five birds. But for the fox, who takes advantage of a combination of rumors and fear, the sky has never been more blue and the sun has never shone brighter.

Basic Lesson

> **Control rumors with timely, accurate, and effective communication.**

Applications for Serious Managers

Ask any employee to name a problem at work and the person will almost invariably say, "Communication." The fact is that effective communication is usually difficult to achieve in any organization for many reasons—poor listening, lack of interest, lack of basic knowledge (usually on the part of both the communicator and the listener), distractions, bias, cultural and language differences, and competition for attention. Yet communication is always seen as a key activity in any business.

Effective communication involves a transmission of information, ideas, and attitudes that produces an appropriate response or understanding. Feedback provides the communicator with an indication of how successful the process of communication has been. When communication occurs in only one direction—as is the case with presentations, large meetings, videos that present a talking head, and speeches in which one dominant person talks at a subordinate—the chance for feedback is minimal. As a result, employees may not feel that they have been communicated with. And when that happens, alternate methods of communication fill the void. Rumors flourish.

Rumors are informal communication systems that do not follow any bureaucratic lines. They begin when the official lines of communication have failed and employees are frightened or insecure. The paradox of (and problem with) rumors is that their transmission method is perfect, but they usually contain inaccurate (if not utterly false) information. When employees have a need to know but don't know, they piece together a story based on what small bits of fact they have—embellished with a good-size dose of conjecture, presumption, or fear.

Chicken Little creates the rumor that sky is falling because it seemed to her to be the best way to explain her experience. In much the same way, most of us need stories that explain what's happening to us and our organizations.

Employees who are not given a rational explanation for their situation or for the behavior of others in the organization will create an explanation of their own. Thus, despite the problems they may cause, rumors usually meet a legitimate workplace need. This is one reason why rumors spread faster than virtually all official forms of communication.

Employees want to hear from their supervisors—the people who will complete their evaluations and who interact with them daily. And they want to hear details and truth. Supervisor briefings can inform the front line of new issues, plans, and problems. Face-to-face, one-on-one communication is usually most effective.

In particular, employees need to know that they can go to their supervisor to find answers. (If they can't, they will look to the rumor mill for those answers.) They need to see their supervisor as someone who has correct knowledge and will share this knowledge with them.

Employees usually feel better knowing the truth, even if it is negative, than not knowing and imagining the worst. It is better to give employees what facts you have and admit what you don't know than to be wishy-washy. Nebulous, arcane, or overly technical "communication" sends the message that you are hiding something.

It is almost impossible to stop rumors completely. But if you are being truthful and forthright, at worst you will provide the rumor mill with truthful information. Indeed, since rumors pass through the workforce quickly, you can even use the rumor mill to your organization's benefit by deliberately feeding it the truth.

A Real-World Business "Tale"

Two small banks in rural Minnesota decided it was time to merge. Since no one bank was dominant, the CEOs of both banks decided that a buyout was not practical and that pooling stock made more sense.

Joe Amos, CEO of Northern Trust, was sixty-two years old. He had done quite well financially, so he was happy to retire immediately after the merger. Amos would have a seat on the board, but Alan Harris, CEO of Minnesota Trust, would become the chairman, president, and CEO of the new bank. Both CEOs agreed that their banks would retain all their current personnel, although some people might be asked to change their jobs or responsibilities.

Joe had some very talented people working for him. He understood that the merger would be a true success only if employees from both banks were supportive and cooperative. With this in mind, he prepared a careful communication program regarding the merger. He was also wise enough to begin implementing this strategy immediately after the terms of the merger were agreed on. This action helped to stop rumors before they even got started.

Joe began by holding an information meeting with his managers to brief them about the merger. He made sure each manager understood exactly why the merger was occurring and what its implications were for all Northern Trust employees, then he allowed plenty of time for people to ask questions and get clear, specific answers. He also knew that if the managers understood the need for the merger, they would communicate it to their employees. In fact, Joe insisted that they do so.

He also prepared a brief position paper in a question-and-answer format, which he gave out to managers immediately following his meeting with them. He encouraged them to make copies of the position paper and pass them out to anyone who was interested.

Alan Harris, on the other hand, was busy planning his role and function as chairman, president, and CEO. He was thrilled with the three titles and wanted a press release sent to the major newspapers as soon as possible. He also spent a good deal of his time planning a retirement party for Joe, who had been gracious enough early on in the merger to voluntarily step aside. Both of these endeavors took quite a bit of time.

But while Alan Harris communicated well with the press and with Joe Amos, he failed to communicate with managers and staff in his own organization. As a result, rumors quickly began circulating.

Myrtle McCutcheon, the secretary at Minnesota Trust who processed the paperwork for the public relations firm that would develop the news release, was among the first to know that a merger between the two banks was imminent. Naturally, she began to tell other people about it.

After seven workdays, there was still no official word of the merger from management. Employees kept asking Myrtle if she was sure she knew what she was talking about. Upset that the legitimacy of her information was being questioned, she began to elaborate on it, thus increasing her importance in the informal organization. And so the rumor mill began.

The story that eventually emerged—created out of fear, apprehension, and distrust—was that Alan Harris forced Joe Amos out and that personnel cuts would be made shortly after the deal closed. There would be no official announcement at Minnesota Trust because the bank needed to keep its workforce intact until the deal was formally closed. After that, the cuts would begin.

As a result of Alan Harris's silence and the rumors that evolved in response to it, four of Minnesota Trust's top managers and several of its staff members quickly sought and accepted positions elsewhere. (In uncertain times, the best employees usually leave first.) This exodus of key people devastated the bank, and the deal was almost canceled because of the bank's sudden lack of high-level people.

In comparison, Northern Trust lost none of its management personnel and only two members of its staff. (And instead of retiring right away, Joe Amos accepted a two-year consulting job with the new bank, coaching the new chairman, president, and CEO on basic management and communication skills.)

The Bottom Line

Chicken Little started a rumor because she did not understand a situation. Rumors at work also begin when employees don't understand what is happening.

Employees are entitled to effective, timely, and truthful communication. This communication ultimately benefits both the staff and the organization as a whole. In addition, it controls the spread of painful untruths circulated through the rumor mill.

In Chicken Little's case, the rumor she created ultimately proved deadly. In similar fashion, not a few careers and organizations have been killed off by rumors. Prompt, clear communication, wisely delivered and managed, can help to inoculate any organization against the easily spread virus of rumors.

17. THE PRINCESS AND THE PEA

Executive Summary

he prince of a tiny European principality is unhappy. Despite his enormous wealth, handsome face, well-toned body, Oxford education, and inherited power, he is still unmarried—and lonely.

It's not that women aren't interested in him, or vice versa. But none of the women he courts—and who court him—ever seem worthy to bear the title of princess.

He found the countess of Vichy, for example, quite charming and intelligent, but eventually he discovered that her secret vices were miniature golf and Gummi Bears. The duchess of Avignon was a delightful companion for almost two years until the prince found, hidden among her possessions, a dog-eared copy of *True Confessions*. For a time the prince began to think he'd found genuine princess material in a Shakespearean actress he'd been seeing. Then, one day, he caught her watching an old episode of *Love Boat* and promptly sent her packing.

Still unattached at age thirty-seven, the prince begins to despair of ever finding an acceptable mate. Then, late one night, as he browses idly through a Hammacher Schlemmer catalog, he comes upon something that gives him renewed hope. "Princess Identification System," the catalog reads. "Tired of all the tedious sorting and culling of possible royal mates? Now you can winnow the matrimonial wheat from the chaff in a single evening by testing potential spouses' kinesiological sensitivity. System consists of an

133

ergonomically designed twenty-layered mattress; one pea of the specially bred variety Mendel's Pride; and a custom-designed oak bed frame. Monogrammed pea $9.95 extra."

Excited, the prince sends away for the system, which arrives three weeks later in thirty separate boxes.

But assembling the system turns out to be a near-Herculean task. The twenty-layered mattress must be laboriously and meticulously fitted together so that all its coils line up perfectly. Furthermore, not only must the frame be put together according to very exacting specifications, but the floor beneath it must be sanded until it is perfectly level so that gravity does not allow the pea to roll off its designated locus. The whole process takes the prince and his staff several days, but at last the system is installed and the prince anxiously awaits an opportunity to use it.

That opportunity arrives only a few days later when, during a terrible storm, there is a loud knock on his front door. Waving his staff aside, the prince opens it. There, in front of him, stands a drenched and shivering—but beautiful—young woman.

"Pardon me for disturbing you," she says with a perfect combination of grace, poise, self-confidence, humility, and distress. "I'm afraid I've run into a bit of trouble. It's my driver's day off, and, unfortunately, a problem seems to have developed with the car's engine." She removes a tasteful scarf from her head and smiles at the prince. "I confess to leaving my cell phone behind. When I'm enjoying the countryside, it's such a nuisance to be answering calls from foundations and interviewers and the like. If it's not a bother, may I come in for a bit? It's frightfully wet and cold out here."

The prince is already smitten. He helps the woman inside.

A few minutes later they are seated together before the fire. "You've quite a lovely home," the woman says, gently brushing back her hair and sipping from a glass of wine. "And good taste in wine as well. I can't remember when someone last served me a well-balanced petite syrah. This is a syrah, isn't it?"

The prince's heart is beating fast. "Yes, it is. It's my favorite of the reds."

"And mine as well." She laughs, softly and musically. "I suspect one won't find any Gummi Bears in your kitchen, or any copies of *True Confessions* in your library."

"Or *Love Boat* videos."

"Yes. In fact, that was my very next thought." She stifles a yawn. "I'm sorry. I've grown quite tired."

"Would you like to spend the night—in the guest room, of course?"

"Why, thank you. I'd be delighted."

The prince fetches her a nightgown and shows her the room. When she sees the twenty-tiered mattress, she smiles and says softly, "One can't help but stand in awe of the skills of marketers." Unexpectedly, she kisses the prince on the cheek. "I'm very grateful for your generosity and hospitality," she says. Then she closes the door and turns in for the night.

The next morning, she limps to the breakfast table looking worn, haggard, and in pain. "Please don't think me ungrateful," she explains, trying hard to smile, "but I found it impossible to sleep last night. I suspect that when the manufacturers filled my bed with goose down, they added an entire goose. Or perhaps your chambermaid has been informed that a mattress is an excellent place for storing a soccer ball." The woman frowns, then smiles again. "It's odd, though. This morning, when I tried to sort out the problem, all I found was a monogrammed legume."

"Marry me," says the prince.

Well, you know how it goes from here. The two fall in love, get married, and yada, yada, yada happily ever after. The pea ends up in a museum, the happy couple sets up a foundation to help people with chronic back pain, and Hammacher Schlemmer posts record profits five quarters in a row.

Basic Lesson

> **The validation of credentials may require substantial effort—but such effort is worth it.**

Applications for Serious Managers

The verification of credentials is critical in recruitment and hiring just as it is for selecting a bona fide princess to be your spouse. In this high tech age, when it is fairly simple to forge sophisticated documents such as diplomas, it is no longer practical to simply accept an applicant's word and documentation—especially since the employer is typically liable for any damages incurred by an employee hired on the basis of forged credentials.

Anyone who needs to be licensed to perform a job should be investigated. Without exception, the recruiter or human resources department should always check licensure, employment history, and education. In addition, any application form should clearly state that falsifying any information will result in termination. And no matter how well an employee may be performing, if any significant piece of information on the employment application is found to be untrue, that employee should be immediately terminated. No buts, no exceptions—that employee must go right away, no matter how much you need (or think you need) his skills. From our experience as consultants, managers, and employers, we can assure you that when people lie about their credentials, they are only going to cause you more serious problems in the future. Cut your losses early and find someone else.

The verification of credentials involves a good deal of detail work and can take anywhere from several days to several months. Therefore, a tickler file should be maintained for each new employee, who should have probationary or temporary status until all necessary details have been collected and evaluated.

Although this advice may seem obvious, in the busy and chaotic atmosphere of most businesses, some of these details can easily be forgotten or overlooked. You must establish policies and procedures to guard against this. Your HR people need to exercise due diligence to make sure that all employees are exactly whom they claim to be. Otherwise, your company may end up with egg on its face, a subpoena on one of its manager's desks, and nothing to tell the court (and the press) but, "This was just another case of something falling through the cracks."

A Real-World Business "Tale"

An extremely large manufacturer of ladies' woolen knits went public in 1997 and had an attractive run-up of its price. An initial public offering brought an immediate price of $24 a share. Within three days the price had quickly climbed to $40 a share, and by the end of the year the stock was an amazing $85. The company's CEO, president, and all the executives were ecstatic and decided to expand their business. This company was an example of a successful family business "making good," and most of the executives were related.

Prior to its IPO, the manufacturer only sold its merchandise to large, upscale department stores and specialty shops. Now the officers of the company decided to open small, single-label shops, selling only their products. Thus the product line had to expand, so they ventured into jewelry, shoes, handbags, and other accessory lines. Soon woolen knits represented only a minority of their inventory. The company eventually opened twenty-three specialty shops in exclusive malls or high-rental areas. In short order, the company's quality reputation was tarnished, inventory control was a mess, and the company had overproduced and was forced to sell to discount retailers. Within a year and a half, the company stock had plummeted and the family was forced to make drastic changes. The company hired a major consulting firm to assist in its turnaround.

One of the critical needs identified initially was to make use of sophisticated computer technology. Although a family member had been put in charge of the company's computerization efforts, the consultants found that the current technology could neither handle the new business opportunities nor solve the old problems. The company lacked knowledge of state-of-the-art information technology and was filled with legacy systems with limited and diverse capabilities and little integration. A national search for a vice president of technical systems was implemented. One of the most important requirements for this position was demonstrated competency in information technology through educational preparation and appropriate past experience. It was essential that the company demonstrate to its investors that it was moving away from hiring family members and was instead seeking qualified talent from the industry at large.

After advertising nationwide, the human resources department received more than 170 applications for this position and selected ten potential candidates. At least three references had to be validated for each candidate, as well as any higher education credentials. Interviews occurred with the director of human resources, then a summary of the interviews, reference checks, and education checks, as well as other appropriate information, was placed in individual file folders. Five candidates were then selected to be interviewed by a subcommittee of four board members. One of these candidates would get the position.

At the completion of the interviews, the four board members discussed the candidates and made their decision. They decided to hire a woman named Alice Connors, who had graduated from MIT with both an MBA and a master's in computer science. Alice was the most polished and articulate of the five candidates with appropriate prior experience. The board members unanimously selected Alice to lead their information system transformation.

After the selection was made, Bob Brown, the administrative assistant, was asked to clear the table to make room for lunch. While Bob gathered up all the manila folders and was carrying them out, a postcard fell out. Bob read the postcard to identify the appropriate folder for refiling it. The card was from MIT and stated that it had no record of Alice Connors. That was all the card said, but it had just recently arrived and was quite nondescript in appearance. Bob immediately understood the meaning and showed it to the flabbergasted board members. Apparently no one had reviewed in detail all the information on the candidates, so thanks to Bob, a major error was caught in time. In the future, all the references on every candidate would be double-checked with credentials verified and reviewed.

The outcome was that Alice was a fraud, had no formal education, and had worked as a technician in only one other clothing manufacturing company. The board members also discovered that two other candidates had been less than truthful on their application forms. In the end, there were only two viable candidates, and a young man was selected who was fabulous with the hardware but far less polished in public relations, which, of course, was not his job.

A modified policy for new hires was implemented with an associated in-service program emphasizing the need to validate all credentials, no matter how long and difficult the process might be or how impressive the candidate might appear during the interview.

The Bottom Line

Although validating credentials can be a detailed and cumbersome task, it is absolutely crucial to any business. Indeed, failure to validate credentials thoroughly may result in outcomes that are embarrassing, dangerous, and financially devastating.

18. CINDERELLA

Executive Summary

hree sisters all work for a large, powerful corporation headquartered in Luxembourg. The two oldest sisters are vice presidents and have posh offices with thick carpeting and fireplaces. The third, who is just as intelligent but far less ambitious, is employed cleaning the corporate offices in the evenings.

As the years pass, the older sisters—who are both aggressive self-promoters—receive regular raises, bonuses, and increased responsibility. But the youngest sister never asks for anything beyond a modest cost-of-living raise, and the corporation never asks her to do more than sweep, vacuum, and empty trash cans. That is okay with her, though, because she spends most of her free time painting, reading, playing the harp, and watching *Good Will Hunting* over and over.

Nevertheless, her sisters are well aware of her talents and intelligence and often seek her counsel on important issues. Although her observations and advice always prove wise, the sisters never recommend her for a promotion—or, indeed, ever reward her with more than an occasional thank-you card or expense-account lunch.

The youngest sister's only vice is that sometimes, after her nightly work is done, she lights a fire in one of her sisters' offices, scoots up close to it, and reads by firelight. Her oldest sister caught her doing this late one night, laughed at her ash-covered uniform, and promptly dubbed her Cinderella.

One evening a year or so later, as she is emptying her sister's trash, Cinderella spots an invitation on the desk. It is for an elegant ball sponsored by Luxembourg's royal family, which will be held the following evening. A few minutes later she spies an identical invitation on her other sister's desk.

Sighing, Cinderella sits heavily in a chair. She wishes that she could somehow get invited to the ball, dance with the country's handsome (and unmarried) prince, become his wife, and never have to empty another wastebasket again.

Later that night, as she settles in with a video and a dish of homemade tortellini, she begins crying. *Where did my life go so wrong?* she wonders as the movie begins. *Do I have to be ruthless and self-absorbed like my sisters to get anywhere?*

"Of course not, honey," says Joan Rivers's voice from the television. "In fact, tonight's your night to prove otherwise."

Cinderella looks up, startled. On the TV, Joan Rivers is smiling at her. "Listen to me, Cindy, can we talk? If you want to go to the ball, then go. You want a gorgeous gown, press seven on your remote. For a complete makeover, press five. For a limo, press nine. You'll need a driver, too, so press three while you're at it. For sleek Italian shoes to die for, press eight. For a copy of the invitation to the ball, press six. Don't worry about the other numbers for now—they're for free dry cleaning and things like that."

Stunned, Cinderella walks slowly to the TV. "But I don't know how to dance," she says sadly. "And I can't just stand in the corner schmoozing all night."

"Oh, you'll dance just fine," a smooth, masculine voice promises her. A moment later, a grinning John Travolta is standing at Joan's side. "I'll give you a few lessons. By the time the ball rolls around tomorrow night, you'll be another Twyla Tharp."

"Now, Cindy," Joan tells her, "remember, everything's a rental. It's all got to be back by the time Conan O'Brien comes on tomorrow night, so we can get it ready for the next talented underachiever. You'll have to leave the ball no later than midnight. Otherwise, the late charges will make your head spin. Are you with me on this?"

"Yes!" Cinderella shouts joyfully, throwing up her hands in delight. She laughs and twirls as tortellini and sun-dried tomatoes rain all around her.

When Cinderella arrives at the ball the following night, she is radiant, confident, and surefooted. Her gown is by de la Renta, her shoes by Gucci, and her hair by Panasonic (via her remote control). Heads turn and conversations cease as she walks through the throng. Her own sisters fail to recognize her, and when she catches the prince's eye, he smiles at her and immediately asks her to dance. As the other party-goers watch, awestruck and jealous, the two glide fluidly across the dance floor like—well, like Travolta and Uma Thurman would have in *Pulp Fiction* if Tarrantino hadn't left the dance scene on the cutting-room floor.

"You move like a gazelle," the prince whispers in Cinderella's ear. "And in case you're wondering—yes, I'm unattached, heterosexual, and emotionally available."

As the hours pass, Cinderella and the prince dance on and on, all the while discussing art, music, literature, comedy, cooking, and film—particularly *Good Will Hunting,* which turns out to be the prince's favorite movie. They are so engrossed in each other that Cinderella is utterly unaware of time passing—until a clock suddenly strikes midnight. Cinderella freezes. "I'm sorry," she says brusquely. "I've got to go."

"Let me guess," the prince says gently. "Fear of intimacy? A sick relative? Reservations on the red-eye flight to Ankara?"

"None of the above," Cinderella murmurs sadly. She kisses him quickly on the mouth, then turns and flees. But as she jumps into the waiting limo, one of her shoes slips off. Before she can retrieve it, the car begins to pull away.

The next morning Cinderella goes back to her lonely, solitary life, and the ball becomes nothing more than a grand, bittersweet memory.

But one morning a week later, as she is pouring milk into her five-grain hot cereal (another of her own culinary creations), something catches her eye. There on the side of the milk carton is a picture of her lost shoe, along with the message, "Have you seen this slipper?"

We don't need to spell out the rest. Cindy calls the 800 number on the milk carton, and soon she and the prince are reunited. He returns the shoe, pays the late charges, and in due course asks her to marry him. She accepts, and they are married in the grandest wedding the country has ever seen, with Joan Rivers serving as the maid of honor. Cinderella and the prince live happily ever after, and she never has to empty a wastebasket or vacuum a carpet again.

Basic Lesson

> **High performers should be given the opportunity to succeed.**

Applications for Serious Managers

In every organization there are potential but unrecognized stars such as Cinderella. They may be assistants, receptionists, or new college graduates just starting out. Or they may be people who have recently changed careers or are first entering the workforce (or returning to it) later in life. Over time, the rewards your organization will reap will be substantial because every time you recognize and support a Cinderella, you encourage the other Cinderellas in your organization to reveal themselves.

Whenever people have exceptional skills, they should be given the chance to succeed, even if—sometimes especially if— those skills don't happen to match the job they were hired for. (If this means changing their job description or moving them to another job within the company, so be it.) Furthermore, managers would do well to keep their eyes open for such people and make sure they get the chance to prove themselves.

We applaud the use of preemployment testing to identify the best person for a position. In many instances, we also recommend eligibility testing, which ensures that an employee is capable of performing a specific job. (Eligibility tests can include intelligence tests, eye exams, physical stamina tests, skill tests, and so on.) Any such exam must test only bona fide occupational qualifications, of course, and may not be used to discriminate against any class of individuals. The human resources department needs to verify that the testing process is nondiscriminatory.

The companion piece to such tests is the job evaluation. Once you've hired people, their performance should be evaluated periodically—at least annually. These evaluations must be based on objective performance criteria. During such an evaluation, it is important to have employees express their own goals and desires for their future within the organization. Are they happy in their current job, or do they want to advance their skill level and/or their position within the company? If they do wish to advance, be prepared to inform them of any opportunities for additional education or skill training.

Ideally, a job should provide employees with responsibility, freedom to use initiative, a sense that they are contributing something of value, a feeling of belonging, and an opportunity to grow. In short, most employees want their work to be meaningful.

Therefore, it is not enough that managers and supervisors share with their employees the mission, vision, and goals of the organization; management must also find ways in which the organization's mission, vision, and goals can help fulfill employees' personal needs and desires. As many managers have learned, in helping employees to grow, the organization thrives as well.

One other tip: Use your employees to solve everyday problems. Allow them to "own" a problem and the process of solving it—even if it is as simple a problem as who uses the copy machine when. As you observe the problem-solving process, the stars will emerge.

It is management's obligation to look for, locate, and nurture this talent—and to focus it for everyone's benefit.

A Real-World Business "Tale"

At age forty-seven, Susan Diaz decided to go back to work. She had both a bachelor's and a master's degree in speech pathology, but had stayed home for the past seventeen years raising her two children. Now both children were in college and Susan was bored.

Susan was the epitome of the volunteer mom. For many years, she was busy from morning until night with her family and her volunteer activities. She had been president of the PTA for six years and had raised more money for that organization than any of her predecessors because of her creative approach to fund-raising. Instead of having children sell wrapping paper and candy door-to-door, Susan had one major fund-raiser a year, each one with an unusual theme or approach—a Las Vegas night, an art auction, a treasure hunt, a murder mystery event, and so on.

Susan's volunteer activities did not stop with the PTA and fund-raising. She also arranged career tours for the children, planned recognition parties, taught workshops in using personal computers, and occasionally assisted in the classroom. Because Susan spoke Spanish fluently, she also served as a translator.

But after seventeen years, Susan now wanted to get paid for her time and effort. She first tried to get a job in speech pathology, but discovered that no one wanted her because she had been out of the field for so long. She was also interested in a job with the public school system, but was told flatly that she would first have to earn a teaching certificate. After four months of unsuccessful job hunting, Susan interviewed for a beginning job as a secretary in a law firm, assisting one of the partners. The partner, Evelyn Naughton, was well known, wealthy, and very busy. Evelyn needed someone right away. She interviewed Susan, was impressed by her, and hired her on the spot.

The small law firm had no human resources department or any type of preemployment testing. Susan was not even sure if the office manager, who was handling Susan's paperwork, checked her references. However, none of that mattered to Susan. She had her first paying job in more than seventeen years, and she was thrilled. Her salary was $12.50 an hour.

As the months passed, Evelyn was cordial to Susan, but never really got to know her. Susan did her job well, and that's all that Evelyn cared about.

One of Susan's many responsibilities was attending the planning meeting for the annual fund-raiser of the local chapter of the American Cancer Society. Evelyn and her husband were members, and the Cancer Society's board had many of Evelyn's clients on it, so she felt obligated to be active in the organization.

At the planning meeting, Susan volunteered to coordinate the entire effort. For the next six months, she did a fabulous job of planning the fund-raiser for Evelyn. She also came up with a number of unusual and creative twists, which resulted in the fund-raiser being the most successful in the chapter's history.

Ryan Fjelstad, the CEO of a twenty-person accounting firm, worked closely with Susan on the fund-raiser and soon realized what unique skills she possessed. Soon after the event, he offered her the opportunity to manage his entire office at a salary of $65,000 a year. She accepted enthusiastically, and he arranged for her to take some management courses at the nearby university. When Susan told Evelyn that she would be leaving the company, Evelyn was shocked. She didn't know what had happened and had to start the hiring process all over again. Ryan, on the other hand, had found a jewel in Susan, who began a new career in a management position.

The Bottom Line

Susan and Cinderella were both able to succeed and excel, but only when they were given the right opportunities. As an employer, it is your job to provide such opportunities for the people in your organization who deserve them.

It's also wise to keep on the lookout for such people—for they can literally be working anywhere in your company. Sometimes stars show up exactly where you think you'll find them; sometimes they turn up in places you'd never expect.

Executive Summary

he Hamlin Corporation, a large Manhattan property management firm, prides itself on keeping all of its office buildings comfortable and in good repair. Thus its executives are shocked when, over the course of a single week in autumn, a large extended family of rats moves into the company's headquarters building in SoHo. Suddenly there are rats everywhere—scampering over people's desks, swimming in the toilets, and stealing doughnuts from the lobby coffee shop.

The tenants in the building are furious and accuse Hamlin of poor sanitation and neglect. The company promises to solve the problem immediately and has its maintenance people make rats their number one priority. But although the maintenance crew sets hundreds of traps and puts dishes of rat poison throughout the building, after three days the problem is worse than ever.

Very concerned, Hamlin executives call in a crack team of exterminators, who give assurances that all the rats will be gone in a week. The exterminators seal every hole they can find in every ceiling and wall, sprinkle a variety of poisons in every office and hallway, and set over a thousand sophisticated high tech traps. But a week later the rats not only aren't gone, but have doubled their number.

By now half the building's tenants have closed their offices until the problem is resolved, and five have filed lawsuits. The Department of Health has cited Hamlin and is threatening to condemn the building. Many of the company's maintenance people have quit in fear and disgust. And when Hamlin's CFO buys a Baby Ruth from the basement candy machine, she receives a torn-up wrapper and a frightened rat instead.

Top management decides it is time to call in a consultant—but no one knows of one who specializes in rat control. Finally, in a consultant directory, they come upon a listing for P.I. Piper, Ph.D., who lists his specialty as "helping companies resist hostile takeovers from competitors, multinationals seeking to diversify their holdings, and verminous rodents."

Anxiously, the CFO calls Piper's number in Orlando. "Yes, I'm available," Piper replies. "I use a pay-for-performance contract based on measurable criteria. If I solve your problem, I get $50,000, plus $5 for each rat observed leaving the building. If I fail to provide a solution, I get nothing." The CFO quickly agrees to the arrangement, and the next morning Piper arrives.

He begins by setting up video cameras all around the building. Then, in multiple locations on each floor, he sets out many small metal boxes. "Wireless ultrasonic speakers," he explains. "I've cranked all of them up to ninety decibels." He reaches into his attaché case and pulls out two items. One looks like a CB radio, the other like a tiny flute. He says, "I'll blow into this ultrasonic pitch pipe and broadcast the tone throughout the building using this portable transmitter. You and I won't hear a thing, because it's out of the range of our ears, but to the rats it'll be like sticking their heads into a jet engine. They'll come pouring out of that building by the thousands. I've set up more speakers down the block, right up to the Hudson River. Watch what happens when they reach the street."

Piper and Hamlin's top managers stand across the street on Twelfth Avenue. Smiling slightly, Piper turns on the transmitter, then takes a deep breath, puts the pitch pipe to his lips, and blows into it until his face turns beet red.

Suddenly, the Hamlin Building begins raining rats. Squealing in pain, they hurl themselves from doors, drop from windows and balconies, and skitter into the street.

Piper blows into the pitch pipe again. The rats screech in agony and scurry across Twelfth Avenue, trying to escape the terrible (yet inaudible) noise.

Piper blows into the pitch pipe again and again and again. As the executives watch, the Hamlin Building empties itself of thousands upon thousands of rats that throw themselves into the Hudson River in a twitching, squealing throng.

Three days later the CFO receives a bill from Piper for $105,050. An attached letter states, "My video cameras recorded a total of 11,010 rats fleeing the Hamlin Building. Please send payment in full within thirty days."

The CFO is outraged at Piper's exorbitant fee for a single afternoon's work. With the CEO and several vice presidents at her side, she calls his office and declares, "We're cutting you a check for $55,000—your base rate plus a $5,000 bonus. Take it or leave it."

Piper simply says firmly, "I can't possibly take it. But I can take you to court."

"Fine," the CFO says angrily into her speakerphone. "We'll wait to hear from your lawyers."

"But perhaps instead you'd like to hear another song I can play."

"What are you talking about?" the CFO asks.

"Well," Piper says, "this whole rat business has caused your company's stock to plummet. It's now seriously undervalued, which means you're ripe for a hostile takeover . . . which also means you probably need me in my other capacity. Here's my suggestion: Engage my services to help you keep the corporate raiders at bay. My fee is entirely performance-based. I get $100,000 for each takeover bid I block and nothing at all if I fail.

Pay me the $105,050 you owe me now and I'll apply the $50,050 difference against my first $100,000 billing."

The executives look at each other, shrug, and finally smile. "Now that's a tune we can dance to," the CFO says—and the Hamlin Corporation and P.I. Piper work together happily ever after.

Basic Lesson

> **Consultants must be carefully managed.**

Applications for Serious Managers

As companies downsize and eliminate significant numbers of employees, outsourcing projects to consultants has become an increasingly popular method of accomplishing work. Consultants, very much like P.I. Piper and his work at the Hamlin Corporation, can be used not only to complete work that would otherwise be performed by employees, but also to do some or all of the following:

* Supplement skills the organization's employees already possess
* Provide specialized expertise unavailable within the organization
* Evaluate the organization's performance, plans, decisions, and internal conflicts
* Take the political fallout in sensitive areas
* Serve as "shadow consultants," assisting management in the organization's everyday functioning
* Diagnose general operational problems
* Provide specialized training and education

Companies that use consulting services, however, need to be extremely clear about their expectations of (and their obligations to) each consultant they engage. No one wants to pay a consultant to be told generalities about the industry, or to hear predictions on where the field will be in five years. Consultants need to focus on what has to be done so that the organization will still be around in five years. Put simply, clients seek answers from consultants, not merely a process. You should assume that a consultant can help you address and solve problems.

It is important to clearly understand exactly what you are buying from any consultant. Any proposal from a consultant should contain, at minimum:

✴ A brief description of the consultant's understanding of your problem
✴ A statement of what the consultant intends to do for you
✴ The anticipated results and potential benefits you will receive as a consequence of the consultant's work
✴ The consultant's overall approach and orientation
✴ The consultant's qualifications
✴ References
✴ Estimated (or actual) costs

It is particularly important for you to understand and be clear about the consultant's specific, promised deliverables. These might include any or all of the following:

✴ A detailed written report
✴ New written policies or procedures
✴ A system installation
✴ An educational series
✴ A specific service
✴ Results of interviews or focus group meetings
✴ A vendor contract
✴ Data shells
✴ New operational systems
✴ Accreditation

Finally, it is critical that both you and the consultant are 100 percent clear about fees and timelines. These terms will be established during the negotiation phase. Some common questions to ask and get answers to include:

* What are the different phases of the project?
* How long will each phase take?
* What will be the fee for each phase and when will it be due?
* What happens if the timeline is extended and the fault is the consultant's, not your own? Will there be a penalty or a reduction of fees?
* What rewards, if any, will be provided for superior performance? For adequate performance? How will such performance be defined?
* What penalties, if any, will there be for failure or poor performance? How will such performance be defined?
* Who will actually be doing the work? For instance, do the senior consultants do all the selling while younger, less experienced staff members do the actual work? (Make sure there is no bait and switch. Establish who will do the actual work up front, before any contract is signed.)

Except in very unusual circumstances, any consulting engagement should be based on a written contract or detailed letter of agreement signed by both parties. Items to include in this legal document are:

* Specific responsibilities of each party
* A clear timeline and specific penalties (if any) should timelines not be met
* Fees, specifically amounts and when they are due
* Specific products or services to be delivered
* Cooperation needed and expected between the client and the consultant
* Independent contractor status

* Client and consultant responsibility for review, implementation, and results
* Limitations

In short, the more details you can work out in advance of the consultant's engagement, the more likely you are to receive what you need—and what you thought you were purchasing.

A Real-World Business "Tale"

Sadie Miller owned Words at Work, a twenty-person communications company that specialized in filling the PR and advertising gaps for large organizations that farmed out most of their projects to large firms. Typically, Words at Work would handle some of the smaller, hands-on communication projects that a corporation might need but that would be either too small for a major firm to handle or would be available from a big firm only at a very high price. A typical client of Words at Work might use a major Madison Avenue advertising agency to produce its television spots and magazine print ads, but would hire Sadie's firm to write executive speeches, press releases, spec sheets, and one-page product reports.

Words at Work was doing fairly well, with annual revenues of more than $6 million. But Sadie wanted to double this figure in the next few years, so she decided to hire a consultant to assist her with her business strategy.

Since she did not know any consultants, she began asking around. Her accountant, who was a partner in one of the Big Six accounting firms, suggested that Sadie hire his firm to assist with her strategic plan. He arranged for her to meet with the head of his firm's consulting division, Mike Pappenfuss. Sadie was impressed with Mike, and from their conversation she felt that he understood her company's needs. Based on the referral and their initial meeting, Sadie signed the general letter of agreement Mike had prepared for her. The company's fees seemed reasonable to her, and Mike told her that the entire consulting engagement would be completed within two months.

Mike Pappenfuss saw the situation very differently, however. From his point of view, Words at Work was a very small account, hardly worth his time and effort. Indeed, he had agreed to meet with Sadie and arrange a consulting engagement for her primarily as a favor to her accountant. Under normal circumstances, Mike would simply have referred her to another, smaller consulting firm.

Two weeks later, when the consulting project began, Mike sent in two junior consultants who had just graduated from an MBA program. They did superficial work, only interviewing four top managers and asking few questions that were specific to her industry.

In preparing their report ten days later, they retrieved an earlier report that had been completed for another client in the communications industry two years ago. They changed some names and a few words here and there, then handed it off to Mike.

Mike presented the results to Sadie in a meeting. Sadie asked several questions about the findings, and Mike was unable to answer any of them. Sadie quickly understood the situation and demanded a meeting with the consultants who had actually performed the work and written the report. Mike agreed to set up the meeting.

Face-to-face with the young consultants, Sadie asked the same questions. Unfortunately, they couldn't give her very good answers either, since they were relatively untrained, had done next to no research on her industry, and had written very little new material in the final report. The meeting ended in a major argument, and Sadie fired the consultants and refused to pay for the project. She also fired her accountant, who was upset and bewildered by what had happened.

Sadie then went to a small, three-person consulting firm recommended by another small business owner. This time she was much clearer in describing exactly what she wanted and precisely what deliverables she expected. And this time Sadie got exactly what she wanted.

The Bottom Line

When the Hamlin Corporation hired a consultant to rid its headquarters of rats, its executives did not fully think through the ramifications of the consultant's suggested pay-for-performance contract. As a result, they failed to accurately assess what his costs would be. Hamlin Corporation would have been saved both money and trouble if its CFO had taken a few days, hours, or even minutes to think through the proffered terms and to negotiate a more favorable agreement.

Fortunately, the consultant provided a face- and money-saving solution. Had he not, however, both sides might have been embroiled in an ugly and expensive legal dispute—all because Hamlin's top managers panicked. Although they acted decisively in hiring Piper, they were too reactive when they accepted terms that they later regretted.

Sadie Miller also managed to avoid spending money for a consulting contract that was not what she wanted or needed. But the initial consulting engagement nevertheless cost her a good deal of time, stress, and difficulty—all of which could have been avoided.

Organizations and the consultants who perform services for them both need to exercise due diligence before agreeing to work together. First, both sides need to determine that the consultant is genuinely able to provide the kind of experience, focus, and expertise the organization needs. Second, both sides must come to a clear agreement on what specific deliverables are expected. Third, the costs, deadlines, and other terms for any engagement must not only be crystal clear, but spelled out in writing.

20. THE ELVES AND THE SHOEMAKER

Executive Summary

his is a tale about a skilled shoemaker who makes top-quality designer shoes for the rich and famous. Bill Gates owns a pair. Imelda Marcos has three. Barbra Streisand has a pair, plus matching gloves.

The shoemaker's products are so highly prized because he cuts the leather for the shoes perfectly and sews each pair with tiny, careful stitches. The shoes are of such quality that he has been able to establish a high price point for his work. (This is a necessity, since it takes him almost three days of full-time labor to make a single pair.)

Unfortunately, as the shoemaker has gotten older, his pace has grown slower and slower. Although the shoes he creates are better than ever, he now takes four days to make a pair and sometimes five. He has been forced to raise his prices, and now only the richest of the rich are willing to purchase his products. His company's profits have dwindled as a consequence.

His directors of sales, marketing, and purchasing all urge him to relax his standards, but he refuses. In frustration, all three turn in their resignations and take jobs as midlevel managers for Florsheim.

At this point the shoemaker no longer cares about anything but making the best shoes in the world. Sighing, he sits down at his workbench. With the purchasing director gone, no one has reordered raw materials, and there is only enough leather left for one pair of shoes. Slowly, with more care than he has ever taken

161

before, he cuts the leather so that this pair of shoes will be perfect—just the thing for Prince Charles or the Sultan of Brunei or Steven Spielberg (all size 11s). The cutting takes him all day, and by nightfall he is exhausted. Shaking his head sadly, he turns off the light and goes home to sleep.

When he returns the following morning, he discovers that the leather has been sewn into a beautiful pair of oxfords, which are superior to any shoes he has ever made. Bewildered but delighted, he grabs his sales manager's abandoned Rolodex, makes a few calls, and in a half-hour has sold the shoes—at twice the usual price—to a prominent Saudi businessman.

Heartened, the shoemaker buys more leather and goes back to work. That day, in a surge of energy, he is able to cut two pairs of stylish pumps, which he plans to complete the following day.

When he gets to his workshop the next morning, however, two finished pairs of pumps await him. Once again, they are crafted even more perfectly and lovingly than anything he has ever produced.

Trembling with excitement, the shoemaker photographs the pumps, scans the image into his computer, and loads it onto his website, along with this announcement: "Introducing Once Upon a Stocking: Shoes So Perfect You'll Feel Like You're in a Fairy Tale." Within hours, he has sold both sets of pumps to well-known Malibu socialites.

Each day thereafter the shoemaker rises bright and early, drinks a double latte, and works late into the night cutting out shoes from top-quality leather. Although he now works longer hours than he ever has and is now a one-person business, he does not stint on quality. He manages to cut exactly three pairs of shoes a day. Each night he leaves the cut leather sitting out on his workbench, and each morning he returns to find three exquisitely crafted pairs of shoes, boots, sandals, or slippers. Within days, he is able to sell all three pairs via his website (www.YourPerfectSolemate.org). And soon the shoemaker is making far more money than he ever has, with far less overhead.

Eventually, though, his curiosity gets the better of him. He desperately wants to know who is making these incredible shoes for him and asking nothing in return. He plans to beg them to accept him as their apprentice so that he can learn to make even better shoes than those he has become famous for.

One night, after he finishes cutting out three pairs of loafers, he pours himself a double cappuccino, puts a pen and notepad in his pocket, crawls behind several stacks of *Foot Fashion Monthly* (which he has strategically arranged in the corner), and settles in for the night.

About an hour later, the window slides open and two tiny, barefoot creatures climb in. To the shoemaker, they look like a cross between E.T. and Linda Hunt. They climb onto the workbench and begin working with perfect concentration, speed, and dexterity.

They are undoubtedly the finest cobblers the shoemaker has ever had the privilege to watch. For three hours he observes their every move—every fluid motion of their fingers, each deft, careful stitch—and makes furious notes in his notebook. In those three hours he learns more about quality and efficiency than he has in three decades as a craftsman.

By 3 A.M. the creatures have completed the shoes. They smile at one another, give each other a high four (they each have only three fingers plus a thumb), and climb back out the window.

Excited and grateful, the shoemaker runs to his workbench, knowing exactly how he will express his gratitude. He spends all the rest of that night and all of the following day making two pairs of tiny (size 3) climbing boots, specially designed for climbing up and down exterior walls. He employs all the new techniques he watched the creatures use, and the result is the two finest pairs of boots he has ever crafted. That night, instead of leather, he leaves the boots on his workbench, along with one of his business cards. Then, exhausted, he goes home and falls into bed.

The next morning the boots are gone. His business card has been turned over and written on the back are these words: "Awesome! Thanks, dude."

The shoemaker never sees the tiny creatures again, but he consistently uses all the new techniques he has learned from them. As a result, his company goes on to make record profits. Two years later it wins the Malcolm Baldrige Quality Award.

Basic Lesson

> **Quality work and service will ultimately be recognized and rewarded.**

Applications for Serious Managers

Both the shoemaker and the elves demonstrated that customers will pay—and pay well—for quality goods and services and that the people and businesses who supply them will thrive.

Interestingly enough, producing high-quality goods and services does not necessarily cost more; it just takes a commitment to be the best in the industry and the understanding and commitment of the entire management team.

A focus on quality must not be a short-term strategy but a consistent orientation—an obsession, really—that permeates the company and lasts over its lifetime. Quality must be regularly valued, talked about, identified, measured, praised, and rewarded.

Furthermore, everyone in the company must be included in the quality obsession. No department can be left out, since genuine quality for both internal and external customers can only be achieved across the board. Vendors who supply the company with parts and services must be included in this quality drive as well, particularly if major services are outsourced. It simply is not possible to achieve true quality if your suppliers are not providing you with the same level of goods and services that you wish to provide to your customers.

All this having been said, it remains true that the customer or end user may not perceive or define quality in the same way your company does. A doctor may have an excellent bedside manner, but may not be terribly accurate in making diagnoses or prescribing medications; nevertheless, he may be seen as extremely competent and receive loads of referrals.

It hardly needs to be said that it is crucial that everyone in your company should understand your customers—their needs, wants, problems, and most important, what they perceive as quality.

Often, quality is defined as added value—for example, features, services, or capabilities beyond the basic ones the customer pays for. Depending on the customer, added value may mean the attitude and knowledge of the sales personnel; customer-friendly return policies; a variety of options or products; durability; hours of operation; expertise and friendliness of technical support people; free delivery or alterations; short wait or turnaround times; or any of a hundred other items.

Companies are learning that customers typically (though not always) do not mind paying more for a product or service that has significant added value. Interestingly enough, these extra features, products, or accommodations rarely add substantially to the cost of creating the product or providing the service. Yet they may cause people to perceive that product or service as high-end or unique—and, in many cases, worthy of a significantly higher price.

Admittedly, producing high and consistent quality requires diligent effort. Any significant quality improvement takes time and may initially cost money. Over the long term, however, quality improvement will usually save money. The concept of cost reduction through quality improvement has been objectively demonstrated. It can be a difficult concept to embrace in bad times, especially if you are under pressure to produce higher quarterly earnings, but that does not make it any less true.

Often when we bring up the issue of quality to our clients, they ask us about the quality/cost trade-off. Our answer is this: There is no trade-off. The quality must be there. After all, when there is no quality, there will be no customers and eventually no business.

When a business is doing poorly, management typically looks for ways to reduce headcount. In most cases, however, management would be better off improving operations and increasing quality instead. Nevertheless, when public companies are in financial trouble, many of them still respond by hiring chief executives that have a slash-and-burn philosophy.

Providing a high-quality product or service with added value is the only truly lasting business strategy available to management today.

A Real-World Business "Tale"

Middle American, a Columbus, Ohio, insurance company and third-party administrator, paid health care claims for more than 2 million clients. Each month Middle American paid out about $40 million and generated many thousands of invoices, statements, and other forms of paperwork.

The company used a single mainframe computer system to handle most of its claims. Although this worked well for some time, the system had not been updated for seven years. In the meantime, the company had created many new products, contracts, terms, and variations. In addition, new federal and state regulations affected many thousands of claims and policies.

Eventually it became clear that the old mainframe could not keep up. It began generating more and more incorrect bills, statements, and payments. Delays in processing and paying claims became more and more frequent. These errors and delays resulted in a 60 percent increase in calls to the customer service lines. For the first time in six decades, Middle American reported a net loss.

The company's board of directors met and decided they needed new management and began a national search. The board hired a new CEO who had a reputation for turning companies around and being tough with employees. This new CEO was from the transportation industry and had no background in insurance or health care.

Almost immediately, the new CEO began to downsize. He cut staff in every department without first doing a thorough assessment. He then gave each department measurable productivity standards. The claims department was told it had to process 150 claims per processor each day.

The staff in the claims department worked hard to meet this standard and almost always succeeded. But to do so, the employees were less careful with many claims, resulting in more errors and more claims that required reprocessing. Worse, some of the department's employees would "lose" or set aside claims that were difficult to decipher or took time to research and process. Superficially, productivity had risen. To an outsider, the company looked as if it was doing better during the first and second quarter.

But by the third quarter, the telephones in customer service did not stop ringing. Complaints and inquiries nearly doubled. The customer service representatives simply could not keep up. By the end of the quarter there was a 33 percent abandonment rate on answering the phones, and the average wait time for a representative had grown to twenty minutes.

The companies that contracted with Middle American were anything but happy about the situation, and their HR people began calling the CEO to voice their complaints. Although he listened to them politely and vowed to look into the situation, his response was to set higher productivity goals for customer service staff. Infuriated, several customer service representatives quit immediately, without giving notice, making the situation in the department even worse. This triggered a second round of resignations. Middle American's HR department, already overburdened and understaffed, now had the problem of immediately hiring and training nine new customer service representatives.

The situation continued to spiral downward, and within a year Middle American had lost 19 percent of its clients. It was now in far worse shape than when the new CEO had taken office.

The board of directors met again to discuss their problems. This time they hired a consultant to assist them in defining the type of CEO they needed. This time they decided to hire a CEO who believed in quality and knew how to institute quality improvement.

The new CEO's approach was nearly 180 degrees different from that of his predecessor. Instead of downsizing, he filled vacant positions. He also instituted a total work redesign project, which included the installation of a new and far more responsive computer system. Although this system required a significant investment, he knew that a full return on this investment would take place within three to four years.

The CEO also quickly determined that the increase in calls to customer service was due to inferior work on the part of the claims department. He immediately instituted an in-service education program for all claims processors. In addition, he redesigned the department's procedures so that the best and most experienced processors would handle all the difficult claims. These processors would not be held to the same productivity standards of the people who did 100 percent routine processing. This redesign helped the department clean up a major backlog in only four months.

The CEO then hired several consultants to help in redesigning the work process throughout the entire company. He took a personal interest in it as well. He walked around and met with the staff. He asked for suggestions, listened to what employees said, and was honest in his answers. He quickly instituted those improvements that were sensible, inexpensive, and easy to implement. These immediately solved a small but significant number of problems.

Staff throughout the company took note of both the improvements and the CEO's attitude. It was obvious that the new CEO believed in quality and was willing to invest in both staff and technology to achieve it. Morale began to improve and people began treating customers better.

It took the new CEO more than eighteen months to turn the company around, but since then it has been steadily profitable. Quality has become a buzzword, as well as the "religion" of both management and staff. No further downsizing has occurred and staff turnover has been fairly low. In addition, Middle American has been successful in both retaining its clients and in recruiting new business. Quality management has kept this company alive and thriving.

The Bottom Line

The quality work of both the shoemaker and the elves won customers for the shoemaker and made him wealthy.

Quality is the necessary ingredient for making (and keeping) any business successful and profitable. If you don't provide a quality product, someone else will, so it is a prudent business strategy to be deeply concerned (and, yes, perhaps even obsessed) with delivering quality products and quality service.

This lesson seems absurdly simple, yet it is one many companies have yet to learn.

21. BEAUTY AND THE BEAST

Executive Summary

A once-rich merchant has lost virtually all of his fortune through some bad business deals. As a result, he now lives in a small house in Connecticut with his three daughters. The oldest two are real airheads, but the third is intelligent, compassionate, and so lovely that everyone calls her Beauty. ("So if you ever get really fat," her oldest sister frequently wonders, "should we all start calling you Obese?")

The merchant makes plans to go to Paris to do a big business deal. "If it goes through," he tells his daughters, "we'll be wealthy again." The two older daughters implore him to bring them back all kinds of flashy items from Paris, but Beauty asks for nothing more than his safe and speedy return. "And perhaps a rose," she adds, "though God knows how you'll get it through customs, so never mind."

The merchant travels all the way to France, only to find that the Parisian police have arrested his potential clients on charges of fraud. Despondent, he flies back to New York and just manages to catch the last train to Westport. But he is so caught up in his troubles that he gets off at the wrong stop and gets lost on a lonely stretch of road late at night.

He sees a large estate up ahead and walks toward it. To his surprise, its doors are wide open, so he enters. He finds a table set for one and a big bag of Cantonese takeout sitting next to it. Hungry, he sits down and helps himself.

Afterward, he wanders through the estate. He sees no one, but finds a bedroom waiting for him, complete with the bedcovers turned back and a complimentary mint on his pillow. Confused but delighted, he eats the mint, removes his shoes, and lies down for the night.

The next day he finds breakfast waiting for him—not just a wimpy croissant and a cup of coffee as in France, but perfectly cooked ham, eggs, and hash browns. He scarfs it all down gratefully, then decides to look over the grounds of his mysterious host's estate.

Outside he finds a large rosebush in full bloom. Remembering Beauty's request, he cuts off one of the roses and, a moment later, feels a hand on his shoulder. A voice behind him says, "Mister, you're in deep trouble now." He turns around. Facing him is the most hideous creature he has even seen.

"Who are you?" the merchant stammers.

"People call me the Beast, for obvious reasons. I tried changing it to an unpronounceable symbol for a while, but everyone just called me 'the ugly millionaire formerly known as the Beast,' so I changed it back. And your name is going to be Dead Meat if you don't explain to me why you've repaid my kindness by stealing one of my prize roses."

The merchant tells Beast of his failed trip to France and of Beauty's request. The Beast nods. "So you're a deal maker," he says. "Well, then, let's do a deal. Send Beauty in your place to live with me in high style and we'll call it even." He pulls a contract out of his jacket pocket. "Sign here and we're set." Terrified, the merchant signs his name. The Beast smiles and says simply, "You may go."

And so it comes to pass that Beauty moves in with the Beast.

Although Beauty has anticipated a life of misery, after a week or two, she finds that she actually likes living with the Beast. He is kind, attentive, compassionate, intelligent, and a good conversationalist. And the Beast in turn treasures his time with her. For several months, the two live together quite happily as housemates.

Then, on a warm night in the spring, with a full moon overhead, the Beast asks, "Beauty, will you marry me?"

She looks away and says simply, "I can't."

"Why not?"

"Beast, do I really need to explain?"

"Beast," Beauty goes on, "There's something else. I'd like to visit my family for a while."

"I'd rather you stayed here with me. You know how attached I've become to you."

"Just for a few weeks. I'll be back by the time the moon is full once again."

"All right. But remember, oral agreements are legally binding in the state of Connecticut. Keep your promise; breaking it could be the death of me."

So Beauty returns to her family. To her amusement, they no longer call her Beauty but Beastie Girl. There is much feasting and rejoicing—so much, in fact, that she loses track of the days. The moon grows full, then begins to wane, and still Beauty gives no thought to returning to the Beast.

Then, one night, she has a dream. In it the Beast appears. He is holding up the contract he signed with her father. "Beauty," he says sadly, "you broke your father's deal and your own as well. Some other ugly guys would sue. But instead, I'm going to die of a broken heart. Good-bye, my darling."

Beauty awakes with a start and suddenly realizes that she loves the Beast. Frightened that it is already too late, she quickly dresses, packs her bag, and runs to catch the early morning train.

An hour later she arrives at the Beast's estate, where she finds him lying very still beneath his prize rosebush.

"Oh, Beast, my darling," she sobs, kneeling and taking his head into her hands. "I'm so sorry. I wish I'd married you when I had the chance."

The Beast's eyes flutter open. "It's not too late," he says weakly. "Will you be my wife?"

"Yes!" Beauty says and kisses him on the mouth.

There is a bright flash of light and the Beast vanishes. In his place is a Fabio look-alike.

Beauty leaps to her feet. "Who are you?" she shouts. "And what have you done with my beloved Beast?"

"It's still me, my darling. I've been under a spell cast by a wicked fairy. But now that you've kissed me, I'm free at last."

"Oh, God, my going away has made you lose your mind."

"No, really. Fairies are constantly putting bizarre spells on people. Think about it: What else could possibly explain pet rocks, haute couture, or the macarena?"

"You've got a point."

"Will you live with me in luxury and splendor, accepting my love and caring for the rest of your life?"

"Millionaire formerly known as the Beast, you've got yourself a deal."

Basic Lesson

> **Honoring both written and unwritten contracts is its own reward.**

Applications for Serious Managers

Not all commitments work out as well as Beauty's, but in business as well as in fairy tales, all verbal and nonverbal commitments should be honored and treated as binding contracts.

This should be considered standard operating procedure for all employees in all organizations. Indeed, we believe it should be part of the code of ethics taught in all business schools. We would go a step further and say that if you wish to manage with integrity, you should view any promise you make as a binding contract.

Of course, many deals are consummated with a handshake rather than a long, detailed written document. Only after the broad terms of the deal are decided on do the lawyers get involved to develop the written contract. In many such business situations, the deal makers need to keep their lawyers on track, or they will get too involved with the minutiae of the wording.

However, even a detailed written contract is no guarantee that all aspects of a transaction have been defined and understood. For this reason, a letter of agreement may serve your purpose better than a ten- or twenty-page document. (At the very worst, there are only one or two pages to fight about.)

Our key point here is that managers and leaders who have integrity often do not need detailed contracts. A simple one- or two-page agreement outlining the key terms or understandings will normally suffice.

Just as the Beast took Beauty's word that she would return, many trustworthy leaders take the word of their employees, vendors, customers, and peers. They honor their commitments and fulfill their obligations and expect that others will do the same. They also take responsibility if something cannot be performed, rather than dole out blame or point fingers.

Trust is one of the crucial elements of effective leadership. Yet trust is not a starting point, but an end result of consistently keeping both verbal and written commitments.

A Real-World Business "Tale"

After graduating from Yale with a bachelor's degree in English, Connie Marx accepted a job at one of the country's largest management consulting firms. She was not sure what career she ultimately wanted to pursue, but working for the consulting firm was fine for the time being.

In her first year on the job, Connie learned a great deal about management consulting. She also discovered that she was skilled at writing reports. In fact, she soon became the office expert in writing and editing, and her skills were sought after by all the senior consultants. Connie enjoyed the writing tasks that everyone else avoided, so she soon secured a nice position in the firm.

After three years with the organization, however, she decided it was time to move on. She wanted to be on a partnership track, and that was not an option at her current job.

Connie interviewed at several national companies and accepted a position at a consulting firm that specialized in turn-arounds. In her final interview with the CEO of the company, the two set the terms of her employment. They agreed to an initial salary, a three-year commitment from the company, and a bonus at the end of that three-year period. In addition, Connie would be promoted to management level if she achieved certain goals by the end of those three years. Partnership usually took ten years to achieve, but the agreement would certainly put her on the partnership track.

Connie took profuse notes during this interview, and a few days afterward, she called the CEO and asked him for a letter of agreement that summarized the terms they had agreed to. The CEO had his secretary write a one-page letter, detailing the major points of their discussion. Connie and the CEO signed it, and she started work the following month.

A year later, another large consulting firm that was on the New York Stock Exchange bought the company. A downsizing followed soon thereafter. Connie and several dozen other employees were given three months' notice.

Shocked, Connie showed the human resources director her letter of agreement. The HR director responded by firing Connie on the spot, giving her twenty minutes to clean out her office and having a security guard escort her out of the building.

Furious, Connie went straight to an employment lawyer and showed her the letter of agreement, as well as the detailed notes she had taken. The lawyer looked at the letter and said, "This is obviously a binding contract. The company owes you your salary for the next two years, plus your bonus. Then there's the matter of lost opportunity. After all, you were on a partnership track and finished one year of it."

Over the next few months, Connie's lawyer had many discussions with her ex-employer's human resources director as well as with the firm's attorneys. None of these came close to resolving the matter. Finally, on her lawyer's advice, Connie filed suit against the company.

After a long and bitter paper battle of charges, countercharges, requests for documents, interrogatories, and so forth, the case was settled out of court, with Connie receiving well over $300,000.

By then, of course, Connie had been at a new job for over a year and was on the partnership track once again.

The Bottom Line

Whether they are formal or informal, written or oral, contracts are commitments that must be honored.

In both fairy tales and real life, effective leaders and managers will always do their best to keep commitments and live by their word—whether that word appears in a written document or is sealed by a handshake.

22. THE OLD WOMAN AND HER PIG

Executive Summary

A n old woman has bought a pig in town and is leading him home. Halfway there, she decides to take a shortcut through a stranger's property and soon comes to a halt in front of a fence. The old woman can climb it easily enough, but the pig will need to jump over it. Unfortunately, no matter how hard the old woman coaxes the pig, he refuses to jump.

"My previous owner never sponsored any training in fence jumping," the pig says indignantly. "My background is in wallowing and grunting. What do you think I am, a racehorse?"

The woman asks a passing dog to help her by scaring the pig into jumping the fence. "I'm sorry," the dog says, "but frightening swine isn't part of my job description. You want a Border collie, not a cocker spaniel like me."

So the old woman asks a stick to motivate the dog by beating it. "No way," says the stick. "I'd have the Animal Humane Society all over my bark in a second. Beating an animal is a misdemeanor with a fine of up to $500. Count me out."

Frustrated, the old woman approaches a small fire that is burning in a nearby fire pit. "I need some help with a stick that won't cooperate," she says. "Would you please threaten to burn it if it doesn't do what I say?"

The fire shakes its flames. "I can't," it says. "You have no idea what strict rules the fire marshal has in this town. I'd be accused of committing arson."

Realizing that the stick will need to be motivated to do her bidding, the old woman approaches a rat. "Listen," she says, "I need someone to do some gnawing. You're a perfect fit for the job. Just threaten to chew up that stick over there, okay?"

The rat shows her his big front teeth. "Gnawing's one of my specialties," he says, "but that stick is made of oak, one of the hardest woods around. I'd probably break a tooth on it. Check the Occupational Safety and Health Act regs. They limit gnawing-for-hire to vegetables, rope, and softwoods."

Sighing, the old woman calls over a wandering cat. "See that rat over there?" she says. "How'd you like to chase her for me? Do a good job and I'll pet you."

The cat looks away in disgust. "Petting's strictly for amateurs," she says. "This is a labor contract you're proposing, and the current minimum wage for rat-chasing is a saucer of milk."

The old woman is now growing irritable and tired. Spying a cow in the far corner of the field, she walks over to it and says, "I'd like to buy some milk."

"Fine," the cow replies. "Do you have a signed vendor agreement?"

"No."

"An account with us?"

"Nope."

"A purchase order?"

"What I've got," the old woman says wearily, "is a pig that won't jump a fence and a splitting headache."

"Also opposable thumbs," says the cow. "See that haystack on the other side of the fence? Bring me over a few armfuls of hay and you can milk me for a while."

So the old woman—who by now is beginning to regret ever purchasing her pig—feeds the cow some hay. She then milks the cow and gives the milk to the cat, which scares the rat and so on through multiple iterations in an expanding sequence of events. Eventually, the dog frightens the pig into jumping the fence and the woman and her pig both live happily—until December 25, when the pig fulfills his mission as the main course at Christmas dinner.

Basic Lesson

> **For teams to be effective, they should be customized for specific tasks.**

Applications for Serious Managers

Before singing the praises of teamwork (which we will do in our next tale), we want to give credit to the managers who assemble the teams in the first place. For the fact is that if a team does its job effectively, it is not only because of the efforts of team members, but because someone in a leadership position made a decision to form that team and then built it appropriately for the task at hand.

Team selection rarely receives the careful attention it deserves, yet the selection of team members can often preordain a team's ultimate success or failure, well before its first meeting is ever convened.

All too often, team building involves selecting the "usual suspects"—that is, people chosen solely for their knowledge base or exposure to the issue requiring attention. Management then hopes that the juxtaposition of these people on the newly formed team will somehow produce miraculous results. This magical thinking may work in fairy tales, but in the real world we've found that a more formalized approach is necessary.

People are enough of a challenge to manage individually, but collectively they defy all known rules. Unlike a chemist who knows the properties of the chemicals she is mixing and can accurately predict the results of their combination, we risk blowing up the lab each time we create some new (and potentially volatile) mixture of personalities. The conscientious manager must somehow assemble a team so that a potentially explosive combination of individuals becomes a rocket-powered vehicle rather than an exploding cigar.

It took some finessing, but the old woman finally provided the right combination of incentives to properly motivate the cast of characters to use their unique skill sets in motivating her pig. Nevertheless, her ad hoc approach, though ultimately effective, was clearly both labor-intensive and inefficient. We believe it is not only possible but necessary to define a more coherent approach to the vital managerial skill of creating an effective team.

Part of this approach involves selecting team members who are most appropriate for the task at hand—not only in terms of expertise and background, but also in terms of commitment, temperament, work style, and a variety of other qualitative (rather than quantitative) measures. However, team selection is equally dependent upon the pattern of teamwork required. Therefore, it is essential that you know the rules of the game before you pick your team members.

Although in theory an infinite number of team configurations is possible, in practice virtually all are variations on three basic models. Interestingly enough, these models can be represented quite well by three popular team sports.

Baseball is a highly individualistic team sport. It emphasizes personal accountability and risk taking and requires only minimally coordinated situational teamwork. This same sort of teamwork is typically seen in sales organizations in which skilled sales staff promote high-quality products or services yet have relatively little interaction with the rest of the organization. Sales staffs are self-reliant and need little hands-on management. At the same time, they communicate both up and down the organizational hierarchy, have considerable competition from their peers, and must be able to take risks and handle failure.

In contrast, football is a highly structured team sport that emphasizes tightly coordinated control, with consistent crisis-response capabilities developed through top-down planning and systematic teamwork. In business, this highly structured teamwork is seen in assembly-line manufacturing, where value arises from operational efficiency and central planning coordinates sequential contributions for cumulative results. The players are hierarchically structured, with authoritarian management and downward communication. (The old woman in our fairy tale used such a highly directive, top-down sequential teamwork pattern to get her pig over the fence.)

Basketball is a highly spontaneous team sport that emphasizes coordination and cooperation by mutual agreement among the players. The sport requires a fast-paced, interactive responsiveness that characterizes consummate teamwork. This flexible, synergistic teamwork style is often seen in entrepreneurial businesses where innovation is critical. Also visible in such organizations is broad-based, reciprocal responsibility for outcomes. Typically, in these organizations there is little advance planning from management, whose major role is simply support and facilitation. The players differ little in status or compensation and may share space to enhance integrated functioning and free-flowing communication. They also, of course, share their identity and risk as a group.

It is possible to use these broad characterizations of the three major patterns of teamwork to tailor teams to meet specific challenges. Process redesign teams typically benefit from the sequential functioning of football-style teamwork. Product design teams and cross-functional teams usually require a basketball-teamwork pattern. Baseball-style teamwork is usually most effective for sales account teams.

An experienced manager may find that certain people are most adept at a specific teamwork pattern. In customizing a team, then, the manager may wish to draft players with an appropriate teamwork style for the project.

A Real-World Business "Tale"

CommonHealth, an international health insurance conglomerate, was facing major disaster from the millennium bug. (Some of its elderly members, for example, were already getting automatic notifications about baby shots.) As a result of the company's serious Y2K problem, its status as the Medicare payer in seventeen states was in serious jeopardy.

The organization critically needed a software patch (what its internal memos referred to as the "Y2Killer") and sent requests for proposals to many software companies with capabilities in this area.

Due to its late-blooming awareness of the Y2K issue, Common Health found most of the major software development firms already occupied with similar projects. As a result, the company received potentially viable responses from only two candidates. One was from SolutionWare, a Washington, D.C.-based company loaded with Ivy League computer science whiz kids with Fortune 500 IT references. The other was from Software Sensibility of San Jose, a Silicon Valley company full of techies with leading-edge talents and plenty of solid hands-on experience.

Since CommonHealth didn't care what the hackers looked, sounded, or smelled like, it decided to run a horse race.

Each firm received a $100,000 retainer for development costs, with the promise of a multimillion-dollar contract to whichever firm reached a convincing, workable solution first. The two firms were simultaneously provided with their checks, unlimited access to the insurance company's IT support staff, and offline access to the existing system, which contained several years' worth of data.

As each firm convened its design team, its managers discovered a total lack of any existing templates to address the magnitude, speed, and complexity required by this project. As a result, each company fell back upon comfortable, previously successful approaches from its own organizational history.

SolutionWare was so serious about creating the Y2Killer first that the president, Winston Rogers, Jr., took on the role of team leader. He personally selected team members from among the firm's best and brightest. The first planning session began at 7 P.M. and lasted well past midnight, with the project list broken out in excruciating detail and accompanying PERT charts that showed the timeline for progress. A command center was established in the conference room adjoining the president's office, and daily reports were compiled there by 10 P.M., when an executive team would meet to assess the day's progress against the plan and to issue modified assignments for the following day.

This executive team consisted of several senior team members, all of whom had both considerable prior experience and good contingency planning capabilities. They kept the process on track and also helped design the bonus program that offered substantial rewards in both cash and stock options for team members meeting their development targets. These project subunits established their own schedules for planning and reporting progress. Any threat to any of the timelines was taken very seriously, and there was no leeway allowed for deviation from the plan.

Software Sensibility convened its team in much the same manner, with its own president, Rob Stevens, getting things under way. He began by outlining the significance of this project to the entire organization and placed its entire resources at the team's disposal.

However, the team that was assembled represented each operating unit within the organization. Unit leaders were asked to each send representatives with a collaborative style, who would then be responsible for communicating effectively back to their unit.

The team was installed in a large room that had served as the conference center. Adjoining rooms were outfitted as sleeping areas, complete with private showers and changing facilities. Support staff was available twenty-four hours a day, as were laundry and food services, the latter of which tapped a wide array of local eateries. Only one meeting was scheduled daily, beginning at noon, over an elaborate lunch and running until its conclusion. No one was required to attend; ad hoc representatives of each of the functional subunits simply gave verbal reports of their progress, which often triggered heated discussions.

Each of these meetings was without a specific agenda, but their overall purpose was to discuss the team's experience with the offline program, its response to various challenges created at the initial meeting, and the refinements the team was working on in response. New questions arose from these discussions and were usually addressed overnight, often by spontaneously formed subunits from across functional areas that shared a common interest.

The company's typically casual dress degenerated with the mysterious appearance of T-shirts with the corporate colors and logo on the front and "Jack the Y2Killer" on the back. One shirt somehow missed the logo printing; it quickly became the prize awarded daily after lunch for the most unique insight of the day, as agreed upon by the group.

The insurance company got its Y2Killer patch from Software Sensibility just 117 days after cutting the initial retainer checks. Although implementation worldwide took considerably longer, the software company's innovative responses to various threatening scenarios at the initial demonstration sold CommonHealth's IT department on its adequacy. (The people at SolutionWare, however, were still several weeks away from a workable solution of their own.)

The Software Sensibility workers finally got to see their families during waking hours and were once again able to sit down at dinner tables, rather than have food brought to them. The story of the Y2Killer project became legendary within the firm, and today a wrinkled T-shirt with a strange slogan still hangs in the lobby, confounding visitors. The design team members each received the same generous bonus while other bonuses were distributed to participants throughout the organization upon recommendation by the original team.

Meanwhile, their SolutionWare counterparts were rolling up the PERT charts and still trying to stop the daily memos reporting progress on the now-defunct project.

The Bottom Line

The success of any team depends as much on its selection as it does on the efforts of its members. Therefore, the wise manager assembles teams based not just on individuals' expertise and experience, but on a variety of other, less obviously quantifiable (but no less important) variables.

Furthermore, since only a very few athletic superstars excel at more than one sport, the manager's most crucial role in team building is knowing what rules govern the project and, thus, which staff members to draft. The three team patterns described in this chapter can provide a useful framework for structuring your own approach.

23. THE BREMEN TOWN MUSICIANS

Executive Summary

A donkey, dog, cat, and rooster have all reached mandatory retirement age in their partnership arrangements with their respective masters. Given that the financial world has not yet conceived of 401(k) pension plans for animals, however, their individual "retirement" programs consist of slaughter, starvation, drowning, and neck wringing, respectively. So each has run away, and together they plan on traveling to nearby Bremen Town to become street musicians or perhaps performance artists.

But it is a long way to the city, and when night falls the animals are only halfway there. Furthermore, they are exhausted, cold, and hungry.

The rooster flies into a tree and from high atop a branch locates a glowing light about a mile down the road. "That's got to be a house," he says. "Maybe we can get something to eat there." So they all set off in search of a meal.

Soon they reach the house, which is large and upscale, and they look in one of its windows. Inside, five yuppies are seated around a candlelit table, drinking Dom Perignon. A cheery fire warms the room.

"Seven million," says the fat man at the head of the table. "Each. Ladies and gentleman, we are now officially stinking rich. And all from a few well-placed bribes and a few words in the right ear at the right moment. What would the five of us do without insider trading?"

The animals have no idea what the people are talking about, but they can tell that they are well off and happy. "Let's sing them a merry tune," the rooster suggests, "and maybe they'll feel generous and offer us supper." The other animals agree, and the rooster, who has volunteered to conduct, gets them started with his best Lawrence Welk imitation: "And a-one and a-two and a-three. . . ." Together the four animals begin braying, barking, meowing, and crowing at the top of their lungs.

Almost immediately everyone around the table leaps to their feet. "It's the FTC!" a man shouts. "No, you moron, it's the FBI!" a woman shouts back. "Oh, God," says another man, "it's probably the local police. I knew that coke deal was a setup." And all five of them go running out of the house and into the woods, leaving the door wide open.

"Well," says the cat when all the excitement has died down, "that worked out nicely. What are we waiting for? Let's help ourselves."

And so the animals do, warming themselves before the dying fire in the fireplace and enjoying much of the food in the pantry.

An hour later they settle in for the night, feeling warm, well fed, and content.

They are barely asleep for a few minutes, however, when one of the yuppies lets herself back inside the dark house. Slowly, she creeps across the living room, past the burned-out candles on the table to the now-cold fireplace. Clumsily, she begins groping for something on the mantel.

The cat, which is curled up on the mantel, opens one green eye to see what is happening. The woman, who thinks the glowing eye is the LED screen on her cellular phone, reaches for it and grabs the cat's head. Startled, the cat responds by biting her hand and slashing her on the arm.

The woman screams and begins backing away. She stumbles over the dog, which lets out a yelp and sinks his teeth into her leg.

Her flailing arm knocks the rooster off his perch on one of the chairs. He lets out a loud, angry crow, flaps his wings to keep aloft, and begins pecking at her head.

Whirling and screaming, the woman falls against the donkey, who has been sleeping upright at one end of the room. He brays in surprise and nips her in the belly. Screaming, she regains her balance and goes running out the door.

"What was that all about?" asks the donkey when her footsteps have died away.

"Performance art," says the dog matter-of-factly. "We should incorporate it into our act."

"Forget the act," says the cat. "Let's just stay right here and live the life of the idle rich. Why work when we don't have to?"

"Sounds good to me," says the donkey, and the dog and rooster quickly agree.

Soon thereafter, the terrified woman makes her report to the four other crooked traders. "It was some kind of specially trained commando unit. They attacked me from all sides at once, in total darkness, and they made all these hideous, animal-like sounds. It must be some kind of tactic to put people psychologically off balance."

"I'm not sure I believe any of this," one of her compatriots says.

The woman begins shaking and blinks back tears. "Well, if it wasn't commandos, then it was something even worse."

"And what would that be?"

"Ghosts. Either way, I'm never going into that house again. Ever. And if you're smart, neither will you."

And so it comes to pass that instead of dying unnatural and untimely deaths, the four animals retire in style in their own comfortable, well-appointed residence.

Basic Lesson

Functional teams multiply your effectiveness.

Applications for Serious Managers

Although the value of teamwork is given significant lip service in managerial training, little attention is paid to what actually makes teams function effectively. Because teams are essentially temporary organizations developed to address particular concerns and attain specific objectives, there have to be some standard guidelines teams can follow in order to increase their potential for success.

The three most basic such guidelines are:

★ The tasks needing to be done must benefit from a collective approach.
★ The team must provide clear value to the organization.
★ The team approach must provide a sense of direction that is meaningful to the organization, as well as pertinent to all team members. (Otherwise it may not justify the additional effort required for team members to function collaboratively.)

Because team functioning is often an alien construct within the traditional hierarchical structure of most organizations, team members may need time (and plenty of opportunity) to establish their own style of functioning. As a result, functional teams are not necessarily efficient at first and need to be given a chance to evolve their own informal systems for handling overlapping responsibilities, collective decision making, and internal conflict resolution. The importance of granting teams this time and freedom should not be underestimated; indeed, expecting effective team functioning from people with heavy time commitments elsewhere will only compromise the team's performance.

One of the benefits of investing in such "evolutionary" time is that each team member gains an appreciation of the skills brought to the table by other team members. Indeed, recognizing how members' skills complement one another, and noting the strengths and weaknesses of each member, become essential for later team functioning.

Because true teams are by nature leaderless, their effectiveness is also determined by their ability to spontaneously rotate and share the leadership role, depending on the task at hand and whoever is most qualified to address it. Consequently, it is very important that all team members be internally recognized and respected for the value of their potential contributions to the team effort. Note how effectively our traveling musicians spontaneously adopted this approach.

Finally, the effectiveness of teams is critically linked to their acceptance of mutual accountability. The specified team objectives should therefore have clearly defined outcomes that are measurable and that have a baseline for comparison.

Mutual accountability is more than just a function of the team organizational structure, however. This accountability should derive from the specified objectives themselves. If a set of objectives does not require a composite mix of skills, then those objectives should not be addressed by a team effort in the first place. Instead, in such cases it makes far more sense to use the more traditional approach, with a project leader who is individually charged with responsibility for the results and held personally accountable for achieving them.

When a collective skill mix is truly required, however, do not handicap the team's effectiveness by appointing a team leader. Instead, stress the team's responsibility for meeting the objectives and the joint accountability they all share.

A Real-World Business "Tale"

Two powerful East Coast law firms with national reputations were planning a merger. The firm of Spencer, Heinemann, and Dodd, which was located in Boston, housed more than 200 attorneys in seven offices throughout New England. Weinstock and Cornell, which was based in New York City, had more than 250 lawyers in a dozen offices across the state. Although the two firms complemented each other geographically, with virtually no overlap in their service areas, it was clearly necessary to consolidate their administrative services and reduce staff accordingly.

As the senior partners of the two organizations negotiated the terms of the partnership agreement, a merger facilitation team was convened to plan the integration of the two companies' administrative operations. The plan was to have these details worked out before closing the deal. No lawyers were on this team, but each firm sent its senior administrator, plus the heads of accounting, personnel, and recruiting. The team's charge was to document the current staffing and budget for each of their administrative units, then propose a three-month transition process, which would result in a consolidated administrative unit with a substantially reduced staff and budget. The estimated savings from the first eighteen months could be used to fund the severance package, which the team was also charged with developing.

The team had no identified leader, but a secretary from each corporate office was assigned to coordinate the scheduling of meetings, the keeping of minutes, and all communication between the organizations. The first meeting was scheduled in a conference center in Connecticut, but subsequent meetings would alternate between the corporate offices. A six-week time frame was established for completion of the merger facilitation plan. The partners of both firms clearly communicated to the team that this effort took precedence over all other assigned duties.

The initial meeting was understandably tense, as the eight participants knew that not all of them would survive the downsizing. The two senior administrators, who had been introduced to one another during one of the early negotiating sessions, facilitated this first meeting and delivered the charge of the senior partners. The managers then briefly described their history with the organization and their operating unit. The senior administrators offered their perspectives on the purpose of the merger, and a general discussion ensued about the potential advantages and risks of the anticipated strategy.

The team agreed to hold weekly four-hour planning sessions, with the next meeting devoted to detailed summaries of the operating units. Team members were then asked to bring to the following meeting a detailed summary of their organizational structure, staffing, annual budget, and operational plan for the ensuing year. All documentation would be distributed to each member of the team no less than twenty-four hours before the next meeting, and computer discs with the information in a standardized format were to be submitted to the supporting secretaries.

When the meeting ended, all team members were engrossed in their own personal strategy to optimize their position. All reached the same conclusion: Their best option for keeping their job was to be as effective as possible in their role on the merger facilitation team.

The next few days were hectic with activity. It was no easy task to pull together the required information and format it coherently. Data was checked, corrected, and refined. Operating plans were polished, spell-checked, and proofread.

When the information packets arrived, they were critically scrutinized. Understandably, people looked at information provided by their counterparts with an especially critical eye.

The second meeting convened in Massachusetts with eight fully prepared and eager participants, all ready to defend their position and undermine that of their counterpart.

The senior partner from Spencer, Heinemann, and Dodd had requested time at the beginning of the session and began by summarizing the merger activity to date. Then he reiterated the great importance of their task. Before leaving, he added that the team's decisions were critical to the future of the new firm—tentatively to be named Spencer, Weinstock, Heinemann, Dodd, and Cornell—and that the emerging organization expected substantial benefit from the approach the team would propose.

The team participants then concisely presented a summary of their unit and responded to a variety of pointed questions that followed. All of the eight people soon had a better understanding of both organizations. Before adjourning, the team decided that for the next meeting, each participant would develop a draft proposal for the merging of their units, including projected staffing and budgets.

The preparation of these proposals revealed many gaps in the information, which each person quickly pointed out to their counterpart. This necessitated many phone calls back and forth to elaborate on the information requested.

By the time the team convened again in New York, team members had already spent considerable time brainstorming a new organizational structure. Although the proposals of each person differed somewhat, they were not terribly far apart. So the team decided that for the next meeting, each pair of counterparts would work together in preparing a combined proposal. If there were any issues upon which the two did not agree, they would bring them to the team for discussion. Team members also agreed to pull together their initial thoughts on the severance packages to be developed.

The fourth meeting was led by the senior administrators, who heard all the presentations, listened to the discussions on the points of contention, and then took responsibility for consolidating the proposals, making sure to incorporate staff from all the departments across both organizations. After a general discussion of severance options, the heads of personnel led a discussion on the legal issues involved and summarized the options that were typically offered. Each pair of counterparts were then asked to create a joint proposal for their operating unit, which they would present at the meeting the following week.

Once again the interim days were hectic, for now each pair had to confer with senior administrators in order to obtain consolidated decisions on staffing and budget so that their severance proposals could be finalized. While no one wanted to squander resources unnecessarily on soon-to-be ex-employees, people also recognized that they were potentially deciding their own fates, so they found it in their hearts to be appropriately generous.

They presented their severance proposals at the fifth meeting, at which the senior administrators also summarized the consolidated merger plan. Both were discussed and the merger plan was finalized. The severance package was expanded to include a bonus for all departing employees who worked successfully to facilitate the transition.

The heads of personnel took all the severance proposals and accompanying budgets and prepared a consolidated version for the sixth meeting. This information was presented, discussed, and agreed on, and the personnel heads were assigned the responsibility of preparing the final summary. The senior administrators planned to present the combined package to the senior partners the following week.

The team then disbanded, not knowing who would stay and who would go, but everyone was comfortable that the new organization would function well and that those who left would be satisfied with their severance packages.

The Bottom Line

The very real benefits of effective team functioning are far too critical to leave to chance and circumstances. Follow a few basic guidelines for optimal team functioning and you will see its effectiveness multiplied.

24. SNOW WHITE AND THE SEVEN DWARFS

Executive Summary

even dwarfs own a business digging gold in the mountains. They have been in the business for years and work hard, but because they lack management skills they are still earning little more than minimum wage. Nevertheless, they are happy and live together contentedly like brothers in a cottage in the forest.

One day a tall, beautiful woman shows up at their door. "I'm Snow White," she says, "and I'm on the lam from the queen. She wants to kill me because her magic mirror told her I'm even more beautiful than she is. Can I come in?"

"Let me guess," one of the dwarfs says. "You're from California, right?"

Snow White pushes past him, slams shut the door behind her, and sits down next to the fire. "Boy, it looks like a frat house in here. You guys aren't exactly organized, are you?"

The second dwarf shrugs. "You saw the mailbox. It says 'Seven Dwarfs. No solicitors.' It doesn't say 'Seven Well-Organized Dwarfs.'"

"Look, I'll make you a deal," Snow White says. "I can tell already that you guys don't know much about managing a seven-person joint partnership, let alone running a household. Well, I've got an MBA from the Camelot School of Management and a degree in home economics from Ye Olde College of Domestic Arts. Let me hide out here with you. Keep me safe and give me room and board, and in return I'll help you manage your business and organize your workflow. I'll teach you some solid business principles so you'll be able to make better decisions, and if you like, I'll manage the household, too."

"Cool!" all seven dwarfs shout at once.

So Snow White moves in and almost immediately things begin to change for the better.

She holds seminars for the dwarfs and teaches them some important business principles. She also solves many of their mining problems, and after a few months she is managing their entire mining enterprise. The dwarfs aren't all that excited about Snow White's business seminars, and there is much sleeping, sneezing, and grumping in each class, but they are delighted to have her run everything for them.

Meanwhile, the queen of the kingdom is unhappy. She still wants to see Snow White dead, but has no idea where to find her. Whenever she asks her magic mirror for Snow White's whereabouts, it always answers her, "She's in the forest, teaching a bunch of short guys about double-entry bookkeeping and TQM."

The queen decides to take a three-week ecotrek in the forest, during which she hopes to track down Snow White. She dresses as a peasant so no one will recognize her and carries with her a poisoned apple, which she plans to give to Snow White should their paths cross.

On her third day in the forest, as she hikes along a lonely path, the queen passes a cottage. On the door is a sign that reads, "Please do not disturb. Management seminar in progress." *Aha!* the queen thinks. *This could be it!*

The next moment the door opens and Snow White steps outside.

"Excuse me, miss," the queen says to her. "I brought you this apple. It's not poisoned or anything, so don't worry. Also don't worry if I look kind of familiar, because you've never seen me be-fore in your life."

"Oh, how thoughtful," Snow White says, accepting the apple and taking a bite from it. "Thank you." As the poison takes hold and she slips unconscious, Snow White's last thought is, *I've got to teach the guys that the plural of "dwarf" is "dwarves."* The queen gleefully returns to her palace, delighted that she is once again the most beautiful woman in the kingdom who is not in a coma.

A few minutes later the dwarfs find Snow White on the front walk, unconscious. They rush her to their HMO, only to find that, under its new managed care initiative, poisoning by fruit is no longer covered. After some discussion, one of the dwarfs sug-gests, "Why don't we put her in a glass coffin and charge people to come look at her? After all, she was always telling us to treat everything as a business opportunity."

That's exactly what the dwarfs do, and it turns out to be a smart business decision. As the months pass, more and more peo-ple come to see the beautiful young unconscious woman. As the business grows they build a souvenir shop, then a snack bar, and then the Lucky 7 Motel. Before taking each step, however, they do the two things Snow White taught them: First, they bring in an expert to help them prepare a solid business plan, think strate-gically about the new venture, and anticipate any potential prob-lems. Second, they make sure to acquire the necessary training to help them sustain each new venture.

One day, a famous young Hollywood actor pays a visit to the bustling tourist attraction, now known as WhiteWorld. He is so handsome, charming, and widely recognized that one of the dwarfs asks him, "Are you a prince?"

"No," the actor says modestly, "but I play one on TV."

"I knew it! Come on, I'll take you to the front of the line to see Snow White."

A few minutes later, the actor is kneeling next to the sleeping woman. He is immediately smitten by Snow White's timeless beauty. With the dwarf's permission and the flashbulbs of paparazzi flashing around him, the actor removes the glass and kisses her gently on the lips.

At that moment the poison begins to wear off. Snow White stirs, rubs her eyes, and sits up. She finds herself looking into the handsome young actor's face, and the two, of course, fall immediately and deeply in love.

Over the next week, Snow White helps the dwarfs invest all their wealth in a prudent and diversified portfolio of stock and bond funds. Then she flies back to Los Angeles with the actor, where the two of them marry. And with the exception of an occasional trumped-up scandal in the tabloids, the two live happily ever after.

Basic Lesson

> **To be truly effective, managers need to participate in continuous learning.**

Applications for Serious Managers

The dwarfs had to learn new skills and techniques to keep their first business healthy and to keep their second one healthy and growing. Snow White taught the dwarfs how to learn new skills and techniques so they could maintain their advantage in the marketplace. In addition, she helped them understand the necessity of calling in outside help, especially during times of significant growth and change.

As the dwarfs discovered, all managers and staff members need to keep up with their fields. In decades past, educational institutions fulfilled the role of preparing people for their chosen occupations. Now, however, with the unprecedented rate of change in all fields, new sources of learning and education have emerged, and in some cases new ones need to be created. New education initiatives must be:

* Proactive
* Business-driven
* Integrated
* Integral to current and future job performance
* Easy to obtain
* Cost-effective for both employees and the organization
* Tied to performance evaluation

Learning on the job is at least as important as formal classroom training. In fact, this daily, informal learning can sometimes be the most effective. Many employees view institutionalized training as boring and arduous, yet those same people are able to view work as a form of learning and on-the-job learning as part of their normal duties. This type of learning can usually be easily implemented and nurtured across traditional workplace boundaries.

Successful organizations typically have a learning philosophy. The general goal of a learning organization is to help all employees and managers develop an ability to learn, adjust, and change in response to the changing realities of the business environment. A learning organization is typically characterized by:

* The existence of a learning culture
* A spirit of flexibility and experimentation
* Respect for the workforce
* Continuous learning
* Knowledge generation and sharing
* Critical, systemic thinking and problem solving

Learning organizations tend to have a competitive edge over more bureaucratic management systems, which are less able to respond to change. The learning organization is comparatively light on its feet and can more swiftly alter its operations as circumstances demand.

Whatever business or organization you are managing or working in, continuous learning is critical. A philosophy of continuous learning will assist you and your organization not only in meeting today's challenges, but it will help both you and your business to secure a place in the future.

A Real-World Business "Tale"

Saturn Corporation, the automobile manufacturer, first incorporated in 1985. The manufacturing plant is located in Spring Hill, Tennessee, and the first Saturn cars appeared in June 1990. The Saturn Corporation is a General Motors subsidiary comprised of more than 9,000 employees building more than 2 million cars. There are more than 380 Saturn retailers employing more than 13,000 sales staff. The challenge that Saturn faced from its inception was to design and build both a new car and a new plant utilizing integrated manufacturing. The company also wanted to develop a new corporate culture (one very different from the bureaucratic, command-and-control culture of GM); recruit, hire, and train a new workforce; develop a new retail system; and most important, make a profit.

Saturn had a huge job creating a corporate culture to meet its business objectives. Training and lifelong learning were placed at the core of Saturn's culture. Included in the cultural design were a labor and management partnership, empowered teams, system information sharing, and a risk and reward system. The challenge of further developing this model was to design a strategic direction; analyze needs; acquire, design, and develop actual training;

administer and deliver the training; and then measure and evaluate the effects of the training.

The strategic direction of Saturn is lifelong learning, which requires going from training to learning alternatives. The training had to support the business objectives along with the mission, values, and philosophy of the company. Competency-based courseware was developed along with a ninety-two-hour minimum annual training requirement per team member. Needs were analyzed and individual training plans, training options, and various types of courses were developed.

Individual training plans had to include federal and state requirements, as well as Saturn's and the individual business unit's requirements for training. Training was job specific, but also allowed for optional career growth. Included in the training plan was a 65 percent completion requirement. In addition, the training was part of a 2 percent risk compensation plan.

Training options included classroom training, on-the-job training, approved books and tapes, college courses, conferences, seminars, workshops, multimedia/distance learning, web education, team-building activities, and on-the-job coaching. Courses were developed on the following subjects:

- ★ Business
- ★ Computers
- ★ Health and safety
- ★ People skills
- ★ Leadership
- ★ Business processes
- ★ Products and process
- ★ Quality
- ★ Technical skills
- ★ Retail
- ★ Suppliers

An educational tracking system was implemented, and training facilities were developed in several geographic locations. For example, one of the largest facilities is the Northfield Development Center that houses sixteen classrooms, four computer laboratories, two computer-ready technical laboratories, a conference center and theater, robotics laboratory, distance learning rooms, media center, and a workplace development center. Several other training facilities were developed to meet the needs of team members. Facilitators, on-the-job coaches, instructors, teachers, and train-the-trainer educators deliver training.

This lifelong training endeavor in 1997-1998 yielded the following results:

* Received highest single quality audit in General Motors's history
* Produced the highest-degreed workforce in General Motors
* Delivered almost $1 million in tuition assistance annually to employees
* Recognized as a "best practice corporate university"
* Ranked in the top three in customer sales satisfaction
* Delivered more than 1 million training hours annually
* Expanded Saturn consulting services internationally
* Received General Motors University start-up support

In a May 1992 speech at a conference for the American Society for Training and Development, later quoted in *Corporate Universities* by Jeanne Meister (McGraw-Hill, 1998), Gary High, director of human resources development, defined the Saturn learning culture as follows:

* Every team member has a training and development plan.
* Training has a demonstrated impact on job performance.
* Training is viewed as an investment, not a cost.

★ Training is driven by the needs of the organization.
★ A high percentage of Saturn team members are involved in providing training.

Saturn's investment in the continuous learning of employees has made it an internationally recognized company, capable of supporting its educational effort. Although the cost of establishing a corporate university of the quality of Saturn's may be prohibitive to some organizations and small businesses, continuous learning and subsequent improvement is critical to the long-term viability of any business.

The Bottom Line

Continuous learning and the resultant change are critical to the health and survival of most organizations—whether they are mom-and-pop operations, seven-person joint partnerships, or multinational corporations.

However, a learning philosophy may not come naturally, so significant effort must be expended to make sure everyone acquires the training, education, and skills needed to keep the business alive and thriving.

25. THE THREE BILLY GOATS GRUFF

Executive Summary

hree billy goat brothers named Gruff decide to increase their personal holdings of grass and clover. Together they formulate a strategic plan that will enable them to reposition themselves among more fertile pastures for greater net yields of greenery.

To do so, however, they must cross a bridge and pass through a series of gates that are managed by a greedy, voracious, bespectacled, nerdy-looking troll of much ill repute. Few goats before them have successfully gotten over the bridge and made it past the notorious Troll Gates without getting eaten. Nevertheless, the three goats have worked out a careful plan that takes into consideration the perils of the situation, the competition for food resources, and the terrible appetite of the troll.

The smallest and youngest of the goats approaches the bridge first. He has barely set foot on it when the troll appears, snarling. "You dare to enter my domain!" he shouts. "Now I shall consume you! There is no escape—no window you can leap through, no higher office to appeal to, no word you can say to save yourself. Even if you excel at defensive maneuvers, none of them will save you!"

Although inwardly terrified, the smallest goat sticks to the business plan. "Go ahead and eat me if you must," he says, "but you should know that I'm the smallest and scrawniest of my family. If you are looking for a real acquisition, you'll want my brother. He's nearly twice my size and he should be here any minute. If I were you, I'd forget about me and go after him."

This logic fits well with the troll's productivity-based incentive system, so he lets the smallest billy goat cross the bridge and go through the gates.

A few minutes later the second billy goat approaches the bridge. He is indeed much bigger than his brother and the troll sees that he will make a very hearty meal. As the goat steps onto the bridge, the troll leaps out from his hiding place once again. "Foolish billy goat!" he shouts. "You've set your hooves upon my bridge. Now it's my turn to set my teeth upon your soft, fat belly!"

"I suppose I can't blame you," the second billy goat says thoughtfully, "but if you are really hungry for conquest, I'm probably not the one to eat. You see, my much bigger brother is coming this way. He's easily three times as big as I am. Don't tell him I said this, but he's quite fat and bloated. I'm just a tidbit next to him. Maybe you should let me continue on and feast upon my eldest brother instead."

Since the troll's long-term goal is total and utter domination of the bridge-crossing market, this argument makes sense to him. He lets the middle billy goat cross the bridge, then waits, anxiously adjusting his glasses, for the biggest goat of all to arrive.

After a few minutes, the largest goat slowly makes his way to the bridge. He is indeed enormous, so big and ungainly that he can hardly walk.

By the time he lumbers onto the bridge, saliva is dripping down the troll's chin and he is panting with excitement. "Aha!" he shouts as he jumps out from beneath the bridge a third time. "Anyone who dares to cross me or my bridge must die a painful, public death! I am all-powerful and irresistible—and you are my dinner!" And with that the troll throws himself on the biggest billy goat, snarling and biting and kicking with all his might.

But the eldest goat is so large and powerful that he barely flinches from the troll's furious attack. While the troll snarls and claws and bites at him, the billy goat carefully positions his head, takes aim, and in a single gesture, butts the troll away with his powerful horns.

The troll goes flying off the bridge and across the water and finally lands hard on his back in a rocky field, breaking his glasses. And with that he runs away, crying and whining about burdensome restrictions.

Soon all three goats are busily fulfilling their mission in the midst of greenery. And as for the evil troll, he never bothers any of the goats again.

Basic Lesson

> **Do not let greed interfere with good sense.**

Applications for Serious Managers

The temptation to bite off more than you can comfortably chew is a seductive trap that every manager routinely faces. Whether managers end up taking on too many projects, entering too many new markets, implementing an excessive number of new systems, or acquiring more organizations than can be feasibly integrated, the decision usually has a partial basis in personal greed. Even though each of these activities can be justified as good for the company, each one also holds the potential to enhance the manager's corporate visibility, span of control, operational budget, or entrepreneurial reputation.

In other words, these strategies offer (or at least appear to offer) managers a fast track to attaining many of their career goals. At the same time, however, they are also a test of competent managers' ability to channel their energies, focus on the organizational priorities, and carry a task through to completion. Therefore, these strategies represent a double-edged sword that can make or break the risk-taking manager.

Here the proper balance (and the challenge) involves taking on what can effectively be achieved without making an overcommitment and, at the same time, without being too conservative, undershooting one's potential or accomplishing too little and thus looking like a slacker resting on past laurels.

While this balancing act in many ways constitutes the day-to-day reality of corporate life, senior managers are particularly at risk for taking on too much, simply because they have the most to gain when their decisions and risks pay off. Pull off one more big deal, do another merger, acquire just one more competitor and you could win that next promotion, get that big bonus, pick up a block of stock options, or have your biggest competitor offer you the opportunity of a lifetime to jump ship and come on board.

The flip side of this scenario, of course, is that people near the top also have the most to lose when a decision or risk turns disastrous—or when they simply put more balls in the air than they are capable of juggling.

It is the rare management text that warns the conscientious manager about this career pitfall. We are told to study *The Art of War,* think outside the box, and be risk takers, but management gurus rarely suggest that we pace ourselves.

A Real-World Business "Tale"

As health insurers began offering dental benefits to help employers attract and retain good employees, they needed to sign up large numbers of dentists to care for these new enrollees. At the same time, to keep dental benefits reasonably priced, the insurers needed to find dentists who would work for somewhat reduced fees in exchange for large blocks of business.

This situation gave Team Dental its start. Several senior managers at a dental supply firm, who found it exasperating that dentistry was still essentially a cottage industry with individual entrepreneurs running small independent clinics, dreamed up the concept of the company. They were well aware of the inefficiencies of the small dental office and understood that this arrangement was not conducive to keeping pace with the latest technology. They also felt that by joining together many different independent clinics, it would be possible to minimize overhead costs.

The Team Dental concept involved the coordination of basic dental services. Its mission was to bring the economies of scale of big business into the neighborhood dentist's office. Its founders began with a business plan built on consolidated offices, centralized purchasing of supplies and equipment, standardized staffing and scheduling, aggressive marketing, and large-volume contracts with dental insurance companies.

Initially started in Pennsylvania and funded with venture capital, the concept was an immediate success with all the parties involved. The dentists welcomed the influx of new patients in a stagnant market that had been oversupplied with dentists. The dentists were also pleased by the way that volume purchasing created substantial savings. The insurers appreciated getting a large group of fixed-price dentists with a single contract. And patients liked the upgraded offices, latest equipment, and expanded hours of the widely promoted facilities.

An initial public offering of the company soon followed, and the early investors had their exit strategy secured. Team Dental took its newfound dollars and began acquiring more dental practices in surrounding states. Wall Street unofficially dubbed the Team Dental concept its darling of the year. A dozen more such organizations arose over the next six months, but Team Dental remained the market leader.

The company then decided to aggressively expand and targeted the West Coast as its next new market because of great interest from managed care organizations in that part of the country. Team Dental's stock value tripled during that single quarter, and because investment analysts raved about the potential, it repeated that performance in the following quarter as well.

Top management then used this highly leveraged stock to purchase every solvent dental practice in the East and Far West whose owner was interested in selling. The company then contracted with still more dental insurers, even though it ended up having to give deeper discounts—a result of the burgeoning competition from other, newer dental networks.

Team Dental's expansion into Texas and the southeastern United States was rewarded by Wall Street with a doubling of its stock value in a mere two months. Soon thereafter, its top management team was featured in several major business publications—in one case in a cover story.

Meanwhile, the rates the company had to offer to remain competitive continued to decline while discounts on purchasing had long ago bottomed out. In the one-week training course for new MBAs destined to become regional network supervisors, trainers talked about the "low-hanging fruit" having already been harvested and encouraged trainees to aggressively innovate the "next generation of leading-edge solutions" for dental cost management.

At this point the growth rate of most individual Team Dental clinics had shrunk to zero. Stock values began to soften. Profit projections, which had been based on savings estimates from the next wave of acquisitions, turned out to be too optimistic. Meanwhile, the pipeline was full of dentists eager to liquidate their dwindling practice assets in exchange for inflated stock.

Team Dental continued to eagerly contemplate new markets, even though many existing offices were struggling to maintain productivity from disenfranchised dentists whose only sense of ownership was in overhyped stock—the value of which was out of their control and entirely unrelated to their actions. Patient complaints regarding service and access began to grow.

The company's stock took its first decline in value when quarterly earnings fell slightly short of projections. However, management expressed great hope for the future because of plans to simultaneously enter new markets in both New England and the Pacific Northwest. Wall Street was placated for the short term.

But the bicoastal market-expansion strategy encountered stiff competition from earlier market entrants, as well as from regionally based programs that had enrolled many of the professionals, leaving relatively few unaffiliated dentists. These could only be won over by bidding up their practice price, although it was rumored that these dentists were the ones that nobody else wanted. This bid for increased market penetration floundered. At the same time, both quality and profits in Team Dental's core markets continued to deteriorate.

Contracted rates no longer covered the company's full overhead, so cutbacks in staff and salary were required. Disenchanted dental staff began threatening to unionize, and Wall Street shuddered at the prospect. Several large contracts were canceled over service issues. Dental clinics in some secondary markets were shut down on short notice, leaving frustrated patients with canceled appointments and no dental records.

As rumors of operational losses continued, stock values slipped further. Dentists who were locked into long-term stock swaps for their practices saw their asset bases erode dramatically. Clinics in several cities attempted to cancel their long-term management agreements with Team Dental, triggering internal lawsuits. In one major market the dentists offered to buy back their practices at a substantial discount.

That quarter's figures reported unanticipated losses, plus a one-time write-off of $77 million. Stock analysts began to question the viability of the "corporate dentist" concept. Stock values plummeted further, into single digits. Three of the four founding senior executives were replaced; they each received severance packages averaging $17 million.

Multiple class-action lawsuits were filed, triggering a federal investigation for fraud. Lending institutions lowered Team Dental's debt rating, and serious concerns arose over the company's ability to pay off an outstanding note. A thirty-day extension failed to find adequate funding, and the company declared bankruptcy.

Just three years after going public, the Team Dental symbol on the NASDQ became TDLQ—and thousands of dentists with worthless stock options filed for unemployment.

The Bottom Line

In upper management, it is rarely considered a good career move to be cautious or play it safe. Yet woe comes to those managers who fail to deliver on their commitments. Thus, each manager is left to puzzle over each new undertaking, hoping to discern whether it represents the "last billy goat over the bridge" or the next to last. Will the current deal be the one that pushes the company over the brink—the proverbial straw that breaks the camel's back? Or can the manager continue to edge a little closer toward the precipice without plunging into the abyss?

Like the troll under the bridge, it is always easy to get caught by the lure of just one more big deal and forget the deal's potential downsides, risks, and costs.

Executive Summary

ne afternoon an executive for CommodiFarms, Inc., gets a startling e-mail message from the director of one of the agribusiness's corporate farms in South Dakota. "Yesterday a goose in Building 12 produced an egg of solid gold," the message reads. "Approximate weight four pounds. This is not a joke. Please advise."

The executive ponders the message for a minute, then e-mails back, "Sell egg to precious metals dealer in Sioux Falls at current market value; deposit proceeds in general operating account; identify income as code 002, sale of farm products."

The next day the executive receives another e-mail message from South Dakota: "We've got a second golden egg from the same goose. Four pounds, two ounces. Approximate market value: $16,000. Prior egg was twenty-four karat; new egg probably similar. Proceed as before?"

After some thought, the executive e-mails back, "Continue with existing plan for disposition of precious metals. Keep me apprised of daily gold production."

Days, weeks, and months pass. Each day the goose in South Dakota lays a new egg of solid gold weighing three to five pounds, which is sold for many thousands of dollars. This additional income causes the farm's gross sales for August and September to reach record-breaking levels. Noting the change, top management commends the executive for his excellent management of the enterprise and promotes him to vice president, Upper Midwest Division.

Rather than appreciating the promotion, however, the new vice president yearns for further advancement. *This is my chance to really rise through the ranks,* he thinks. *If I can only find out what makes this goose tick I can patent it, send it over to our genetic engineering people, and have them replicate it through hormone shots or gene splicing or whatever. Soon we'll have whole farms of geese laying golden eggs. If I do this right, I'll be president of CommodiFarms in a couple of years.*

Shaking with excitement and avarice, the vice president puts in a call to the farm director in South Dakota. "I want to know everything about this goose," he tells her. "Her place of birth, health history, heart rate, and blood type, assuming geese have blood types. I want to know her reproductive system inside and out. Is there anything unusual about her ovaries, uterus, fallopian tubes. Do geese have fallopian tubes? Whatever reproductive parts geese have, I want to become the world's leading expert on them—and on hers in particular."

After a long pause, the director says softly, "I'd advise against that."

The vice president replies sharply, "Your advice has been noted. Now please do what I said."

"Excuse me, sir, but the only way to really obtain all the information you're after is to kill the goose."

By now the vice president's brain is swimming with two visions. The first is of building after building filled with gold-producing geese; the second is of the president's sunny, expansive office on the fifty-first floor of the CommodiFarms building. "That's fine," he says curtly. "Slit her throat if you need to. Just let me know what you find."

So the director of the farm has the goose slaughtered, and two zoologists from South Dakota State University are brought in to look for anything unusual. But after hours of examining the corpse, all they can say is, "You've given us a completely normal dead goose."

With the goose gone, the farm's monthly income suddenly falls by a half million dollars—a drop that the vice president cannot easily account for. Within four months he is forced to resign from CommodiFarms in disgrace—a victim of his own shortsightedness.

Basic Lesson

> **Do not undervalue the means of production.**

Applications for Serious Managers

While greed may have been this foolish executive's motive, just as in our last tale, his actual fatal error lay not so much in wanting more, but in appreciating only the product and failing to appropriately value the means of production.

Never once in the numerous versions of this tale does anyone think of feeding this very talented goose better food, perhaps to get bigger (or more frequent) eggs. No one considers moving it into better quarters so that it stays warm, dry, and healthy and thus can live a long time and lay lots of golden eggs. No one suggests investing in a security system or bodyguard to protect the exceptional fowl. The goose's owner gets wealthy, but this wealth is never associated with the well-being of the goose, only with the value of the eggs she produces.

This dissociation of what is produced from how it is produced (and by whom) is an all-too-common management error. Perhaps it is a holdover from the early days of automation, when any warm body could perform simple, repetitive assembly-line tasks and everyone was thus replaceable.

But those days are long gone. We now live in the era of knowledge workers—employees who, regardless of their job, accumulate a wealth of pertinent information. What too many employers fail to understand is that this acquired knowledge creates a value that rivals the value of the product itself. Indeed, the two are intimately intertwined.

In service industries, ignoring the production capabilities of the frontline staff is especially risky, for employees essentially are the products. Although Disney, Nordstrom's, and the Ritz-Carlton Hotel may tout their in-house management training programs as the source of their legendary service, the frontline staff actually deserves most of the credit, for these employees are the vehicles for delivering that service. Unless those people are dedicated, motivated, and adequately rewarded for delivering the service they have been trained to provide, those renowned programs become nothing more than employee orientations.

While the value of frontline staff to the success of an enterprise is a simple concept to verbalize, the challenge, as usual, is in the execution. No matter how many apocryphal business school case studies demonstrate the impact of employee-led quality circles, the message that too many managers send their employees is, "We don't care about you; we just care about getting the job done adequately and efficiently."

It is a sad but frequent irony that when an organization in trouble responds with cutbacks, layoffs, and downsizing, Wall Street often upgrades its stock price. Yet this direct attack on the means of production holds little hope for improving the product, but merely serves to reduce the cost of producing it. This may seem to be a sound decision on the surface, but in so doing, senior management often takes on the same risk the executive did in slaughtering the goose.

"Chainsaw" Al Dunlap, the ex-CEO of Sunbeam, provides us with a valuable lesson in this regard. Few leaders have received as much publicity for the slash-and-burn approach to management as Dunlap. In his two-year tenure at Sunbeam, he closed eighteen of twenty-six plants and laid off nearly half the Sunbeam work-force. While initially Wall Street rewarded his efforts to cut fat with increased stock value, it was just as eager to turn on him when the promised profits did not materialize. After fewer than 600 business days, Dunlap got the ax for missing what should be an obvious linkage: The products you sell to make your profits have to be made by somebody.

A Real-World Business "Tale"

BestPlan was a decades-old Midwestern HMO that had recently fallen on hard times. For one thing, there was a backlash of anti-managed care sentiment in the media, and both political parties were promising to control the evils perpetrated on the public by demonic HMO administrators. For another, employers wanted their costs lowered, even though state and federal regulation steadily raised the cost of doing business. Furthermore, virtually every competing plan now offered members a choice of physicians as well as open access to specialists; as a result, BestPlan was getting squeezed by dropping enrollments.

BestPlan's board of directors considered replacing its current CEO, a physician who had started the company twenty years ago, back in the days when the words *HMO* and *managed care* didn't scare people. In secret sessions, the board interviewed a candidate for the job, a financial consultant from a major accounting firm who had impressed many board members during a recent audit.

During the interviews, the candidate laid out a surprisingly detailed plan for freezing wages wherever possible, combining and eliminating a variety of staff positions, replacing nurses with medical assistants and nurses' aides, placing an annual cap on the number of promotions any unit could grant to its staff, filling vacant positions with less experienced (and less costly) employees, and eliminating specialty physicians by contracting out for those services. Although the consultant's financial projections were cursory, they generally demonstrated that the organization could eliminate the current deficit and break even in the years to come (as long as the situation did not deteriorate further). In his projections, the consultant also roughed out a contingency plan that described a second round of downsizing in case the situation did not stabilize.

The board was nearly unanimous in its endorsement of the consultant for the CEO position. There was one exception, however: a retired schoolteacher who represented the community. She asked a critical question: "How will reducing the costs increase enrollment in BestPlan?"

Surprisingly, the candidate's contingency plans did not even begin to address this issue. The board immediately got the point that enrollment was a function of the doctors, nurses, and other staff of BestPlan. If enrollment was the problem, then reducing costs at staff's expense was not a solution, but only a temporary plateau on the death spiral. In fact, the CEO's plan would have resulted in the departure of some of BestPlan's most talented people, as well as seriously lowered morale among the downsized survivors who chose to stay.

The board decided to put its candidate search aside and instead focus on the results of member satisfaction surveys done in the past two years, as well as on the data that had been collected on why members dropped out of BestPlan. What they discovered was a long list of complaints from members about access to appointments, availability of services, and responsiveness of staff.

All of these issues were operational in nature, and board members realized with a shock that none of them had been addressed in the plans of the CEO candidate. In fact, the approach the consultant suggested would have further aggravated many of the issues by further overextending staff and disrupting systems that were already dysfunctional.

At this point the board's course was clear—and it became equally clear that the current CEO was well positioned to carry it out.

Changes that had been discussed for years, but had been resisted by staff because they were inconvenient, were finally introduced. Hours were extended to include 7:00 A.M. appointment times; evening clinics were added for working parents; and weekend hours were expanded from Saturday morning to all day Saturday, plus Sunday morning. In some clinics staff were added, while in others more effective supervision improved staff efficiency. These changes eliminated a great deal of frustration for patients.

The message that management delivered to staff along with these changes was straightforward: This is what our customers want, and if we are to keep them—and our jobs—they will have to be implemented. The staff, understanding the critical position the organization was in, as well as the professional jeopardy they all faced, accepted the changes with only minor objections.

Ultimately, the HMO's staffing and budget both increased as the result of these changes. So did patient enrollment—significantly.

Almost immediately, the additional staffing created additional capacity that, like a vacuum, was quickly filled by patient need. The ability to schedule appointments more easily, get in to see a physician more quickly, and access clinic services more conveniently made members happy. These changes caused a number of old members to return, pleased to once again see the physicians they had dealt with for years. New members joined as well, frustrated with the inconvenience of overtaxed systems at competing health plans.

It took two quarters for the changes to become fully apparent, but by that time break-even was imminent and profits were forecast for the end of the year. By the time December 31 arrived, patient satisfaction was at an all-time high. The board wisely viewed the profits that were beginning to develop as interest earned on BestPlan's greatest investment, its staff.

The Bottom Line

The health of an organization depends on the successful performance of its workforce. In a labor environment in which all work is rapidly becoming knowledge work, this in turn depends on staff being recognized, appreciated, and appropriately valued by management.

It also means creating a feeling of safety. Staffs need to feel that if they perform well and contribute to the organization they will not be "rewarded" with a pink slip as soon as times get tough. Furthermore, managers need to understand that laying off staff not only undermines the confidence and trust of the remaining workforce, but also causes the organization to lose the knowledge accumulated in the heads of the workers walking out the door.

It is a classic mistake of shortsighted managers to jeopardize their product by undervaluing the means of its production. Not only is this attitude somewhat inhumane, but it can set off a downward spiral leading ultimately to insolvency.

Some simple attention to the needs of staff—and a willingness to treat them like the valuable assets they are—can go a long way toward solving (and preventing) a variety of organizational problems.

Executive Summary

 suburb in a distant fiefdom has hit on hard times. The carriage assembly plant, which has long been the basis of the local economy, has been closed since spring, driven out of business by competition from a far eastern kingdom.

When the plant closing was first rumored, the mayor advocated planting gardens, rationing food supplies, and storing nonperishables for later use. But most people ignored his advice, convinced that a white knight would come forth to bail them out. That never happened, however, and now times are dire indeed.

As winter nears, starvation looms for many of the town's residents. Yet among others, entrenchment and food hoarding are apparent. The mayor knows that some of these people have accumulated substantial reserves but are not inclined to share any of their assets—or even admit publicly that they exist.

In response, the mayor holds a series of public forums in which he urges collaborative efforts and interdependence. Preoccupied with their own troubles, however, most people ignore the presentations and stay home.

Concerned that the town will not make it through the winter, the mayor then builds a team with the requisite skills to help its residents survive the difficult times ahead. He selects an ex-quartermaster to help with inventory, a CPA to count the beans, a chef to design low-cost yet nutritional menus, and a warehouse foreman to counsel on food storage and preservation. But although the team dutifully develops a detailed and potentially effective plan of action, the citizens of the town—more concerned with their own families than with their civic duty—fail to participate in significant numbers.

As food shortages begin to be reported, a member of the town council proposes a resolution obligating families to surrender one-half of their current food supply, to be centrally managed for the good of the entire community. The other council members are ready to approve the measure, but the mayor, realizing that such an arrangement would result in a huge uproar, if not outright revolution, asks the council to table the resolution for a few days. "There's one other strategy I'd like to try before we resort to central planning," he says.

Two days later, at the monthly town meeting, the mayor announces that he has acquired a new form of nutritional technology that promises to resolve the community's threatened food shortage. "I've just returned from the food services industry trade show," he says, "where I learned of a cutting-edge technique for making a delicious and highly nutritious soup from common nails. This soup can provide our families with the key minerals, vitamins, and other nutrients we need all winter long." Amid much hooting and heckling from the crowd, the mayor adds, "Fortunately, because our economic troubles have prevented the construction of our community bingo parlor and bowling alley, nails are in abundance." He announces that a community cook-off will take place the following evening, at which he will personally supervise the preparation and distribution of enough soup to feed the entire town throughout the coming winter. "Everyone bring your biggest pot," he says, "and I'll send you home with it filled with delicious and satisfying soup—and a method for keeping it full until spring."

Although the populace doubts that the mayor will be able to walk his talk, everyone in the suburb shows up the following evening, cooking pots in hand, curious about the secret behind nail soup. All of these pots are quickly set to boiling. The mayor then hands out thousands of nails and has people add a ration of them to each pot—the bigger the pot, the more nails.

As steam begins to rise from the pots, the mayor nods and smiles. "The soup is going to be every bit as good as what I sampled at the trade show. But a little bit of salt and pepper in each pot will enhance the flavor. It's a shame we don't have any." Over the next few minutes, however, several citizens manage to find and deliver supplies of both spices adequate to the demand.

As the soup begins bubbling briskly, the mayor takes a taste. "Superb," he says, "but an onion or two in each pot will make this soup truly first-rate." Within a few minutes, well over a hundred onions appear miraculously from residents' pantries. These are quickly cut up and added to the pots.

"You know," the mayor says thoughtfully, stirring one of the pots, "if only we had a few carrots and potatoes, we'd be able to create some of the finest nail soup this kingdom has ever known." Soon quantities of both are discovered in people's kitchens and root cellars, and they are promptly sliced and contributed to the pots.

As mouth-watering odors waft forth from the pots, the mayor announces, "It seems to me that this soup would be suitable for the Queen herself, if only a bit of meat could be added." In response, many of the town's citizens recall spare joints of mutton and unused stew meat that they are willing to contribute. These, too, are added and the pots are boiled for a few minutes more.

Finally, the mayor pronounces the soup done and the pots are then distributed, one per household. The mayor instructs everyone to maintain them at a low simmer through the winter, adding occasional vegetables or meat according to individual taste—but never, ever removing the nails from the bottom. He also encourages families to share their soup—and soup ingredients—with one another so that a variety of different recipes can be developed.

Thus the community is sustained through the winter. Furthermore, nail soup becomes a favorite regional dish, passed down from generation to generation, with the added advice that "it's what you add that makes the difference." A subsequent cookbook, *Cooking With Nails*, sells well enough to spawn a sequel, *Low-Fat Cooking With Nails*, and to make the suburb into a tourist attraction. Soon people are coming from all over the kingdom to the many inns and B&B's that specialize in authentic nail soup. And the local economy thrives once again.

Basic Lesson

> **Effective leaders adapt their management approach to best suit the particular situation.**

Applications for Serious Managers

Although leadership is a critical focus of every MBA program, there are no curricula that actually develop leaders. Rather, they merely teach some of the skills that leaders require, such as strategic planning, decision making, and communication.

Charles M. Farkas and Suzy Wetlaufer made a large contribution to our understanding of leadership in their article "The Way

Chief Executive Officers Lead," which appeared in the May/June 1996 issue of *Harvard Business Review*. Farkas and Wetlaufer interviewed 160 CEOs from a variety of organizations and industries throughout the world in an attempt to identify the attitudes, activities, and behaviors that characterized their (supposedly) unique management approach.

To their surprise, among all of these leaders, they discovered no more than five distinct approaches to management. Farkas and Wetlaufer called these five approaches strategy, change, human assets, box, and expertise.[1]

★ The **strategy** approach focuses on future positioning based on current realities, rather than on day-to-day operations. Leaders who use this approach spend 80 percent of their time dealing with (or thinking about) customers, competitors, market trends, and technological advances.

★ The **change** approach, which is common in rapidly evolving industries, requires creating an environment supportive to continual reinvention of the basic business. Leaders employing this approach spend much of their time in the field to keep abreast of the latest innovations. They typically devote considerable attention to communicating to their colleagues and subordinates a philosophy that embraces change.

★ The **human assets** approach emphasizes a proximity to the marketplace and values the behaviors and attitudes of a broadly trained spectrum of staff. Leaders who take this approach focus their energies on personnel issues, carefully recruiting, training, promoting, and evaluating the performance of staff.

★ The **box** approach is most frequently used in highly regulated industries such as banking and insurance. Leaders who work

---

[1]Charles M. Farkas and Suzy Wetlaufer, "The Ways Chief Executive Officers Lead," *Harvard Business Review* (May-June, 1996).

with a box approach desire to provide a uniform, predictable experience for their customers. Thus they spend much of their time establishing and communicating both formal and informal rules, regulations, policies, and procedures, which are to be followed explicitly.

★ Lastly, the **expertise** approach involves the selection, support, nurturing, and promotion of a particular area of expertise that provides a competitive advantage for the organization. Leaders who take an expertise approach spend the majority of their time cultivating that expertise through analysis, research, staff and product development, and meetings with other experts.

Significantly, Farkas and Wetlaufer noted that these approaches were not ingrained in each individual as some function of their personality. Rather, each person's current approach was specifically selected to meet the current demands of their organization. When those demands changed, capable leaders modified their management approach as appropriate.

As we all learned in management training, the role of leadership is threefold:

1. To develop a clear purpose and direction for the organization, with specific goals
2. To build organizational commitment to those goals
3. To establish consistent organizational systems to support the goals

The five approaches to management described previously are all used by leaders to deliver this clarity, commitment, and consistency. Although the mayor in our tale struggled to find the key to unlocking the hoarded food, he eventually got it right. Choosing the right approach at the right time is the essence of true leadership.

A Real-World Business "Tale"

Costanzo Construction had been a successful business for two decades. For years, Costanzo had held long-term arrangements with major contractors to build many of southern California's ubiquitous housing tracts. After its founder, Joe Costanzo, died, his oldest son, Joe Jr., took over the business and the four other Costanzo brothers continued in their roles as foremen. But there was no change in the winning approach the family had followed for as long as any of the sons could remember.

Each son managed a separate project and had built good relationships with trusted supervisors. The company employed crews of migrant laborers, but many of these people had worked with Costanzo for years as well. A well-defined team approach had been developed, with six laborers needed on each house, so project staffing was a simple matter of multiplying the number of houses by six.

Little Joe (as family members called him) was responsible for logistics across all projects. He also managed a separate crew that was in charge of delivering all necessary equipment and supplies. Long experience had helped the company develop its supply lists, which detailed how much was needed, how often, in what quantities, and so on. All of this was coordinated at dinner on Sunday night at Mama Costanzo's, a family tradition.

Little Joe had worked closely with his father on these details, as well as on budgets and salaries, and together they had gotten these as close to a science as they could. Nevertheless, the company was now facing a problem: The big projects just weren't there anymore. A recession in the aerospace industry had chased away the money; Orange County was bankrupt; and interest rates were not kind to anyone looking for a new mortgage. For the first time ever, the company had to lay off some of its general carpenters, and the supervisors had taken all the unpaid vacation they could financially tolerate.

All the work now was in remodeling, and it was slow in coming. The Costanzos found that it wasn't very profitable, either. Their staffing was never quite right, and they began wasting a lot of time getting the correct supplies, which varied from project to project. The foremen were also frustrated at having to travel between multiple, scattered projects. Meanwhile, some of the work teams were performing poorly when they were left unsupervised for up to a half day at a time. Benny, the youngest brother, was beginning to talk about working for someone else. Sunday night dinners were dragging into late evening as the brothers sought to keep all the projects straight.

It was all too obvious to Little Joe that none of the treasured family formulas seemed to work anymore, so the following Sunday he made a proposal to his brothers. If remodeling was the only business to be had, they needed to learn to do it as efficiently as they used to do new construction. He suggested that each brother do no more than two things at a time: manage one project currently under construction and plan his next one. Each foreman would customize his work team for each specific project, and each would also be responsible for tailoring his own list of equipment and supplies. Little Joe would be responsible for managing a flexible pool of carpenters and for keeping a central storage area stocked with all the equipment and supplies likely to be needed. In addition, he would track all the projects and assign the next one for planning. Little Joe also took on the role of salesman— a role that had never been needed before but now was critical.

Benny decided to stay with the business and quickly developed a real talent for the customized projects. But the youngest of the brothers, Tony, could never get the hang of the new way of working; after eight months, with his family's blessing, he went into business with his father-in-law. Several supervisors were let go, but two others who had years of experience in custom remodeling work were added.

The contractors for whom the company had built tract homes turned out to be good sources of referrals, and the brothers' newly developed approach soon won them praise from their satisfied customers, so more business followed. Within a year, the company's profits became almost as good as they had been on straight construction.

Little Joe felt comfortable with this new approach as he packed away the old schedules and now-useless lists of staff, supplies, and equipment. But he marked the box well because he knew that the next shift in the market might require Costanzo Construction to revert back to its previous approach.

The Bottom Line

Leadership is not a personality trait or a programmatic approach to attaining a goal, but a cultivated mode of action, consciously selected to fit a specific situation.

The mayor in our fairy tale found the expertise approach most effective, but only after trying—and failing at—other approaches. Little Joe Costanzo gave up the comfort and familiarity of the box approach to take on the uncertainty of the change approach. Both men were required by circumstances to consciously change their management approaches; both succeeded only because they were observant enough and wise enough to realize that such a change was necessary.

It is the wise, not to mention effective, leader who responds to the environmental forces in the marketplace and tailors a management style accordingly.

SOURCES OF THE FAIRY TALES

Aesop's Fables
  The Boy Who Cried Wolf
  The Goose With the
    Golden Eggs
  The Hare and the Tortoise

Andersen, Hans Christian
  The Emperor's New Clothes
  The Little Match Girl
  The Princess and the Pea
  The Steadfast Tin Soldier
  The Ugly Duckling

Beaumont, Madame de
  Beauty and the Beast

The Brothers Grimm
  The Bremen Town
    Musicians
  The Elves and the
    Shoemaker
  Hansel and Gretel
  Rumpelstiltskin
  Snow White and the
    Seven Dwarfs

The Twelve Dancing
  Princesses

Perrault, Charles, *Tales of Past
  Times*
  Cinderella
  Little Red Riding Hood
  Puss in Boots
  Sleeping Beauty

Southey, Robert
  Goldilocks and the
    Three Bears

Traditional Czech
  Nail Soup

Traditional English
  Chicken Little
  Jack and the Beanstalk
  The Old Woman and
    Her Pig
  The Pied Piper
  The Three Little Pigs

Traditional Scandinavian
  The Three Billy Goats Gruff

INDEX

241

ABOUT THE AUTHORS

Gloria Gilbert Mayer is a corporate consultant, trainer, and writer whose specialties include team building, communications, and managing in times of chaos. She is also president of the Institute for Health Care Advancement, a nonprofit educational foundation in Whittier, California.

Prior to becoming a full-time consultant, Gloria was president and chief operating officer of Friendly Hills HealthCare Network, a $600 million medical group in southern California. Her previous books include *2001 Tips for Working Mothers* (Morrow: New York, 1983); *The Middle Manager in Primary Care Nursing* (Springer: New York, 1982); *Kids' Chic*, with Mary Ellen Mc-Glone (Evans: New York, 1984); *Making Capitation Work* (Aspen: Gaithersburg, Maryland, 1996); *Ambulatory Care Management and Practice* (Aspen: Gaithersburg, Maryland, 1982); and *Patient Care Delivery Models* (Aspen: Gaithersburg, Maryland, 1990).

Thomas Mayer has an MBA and has served as CEO of Strategic HealthCare Management, a firm specializing in medical mergers and acquisitions. He has published *A Guide to Forming Physician Networks*, with Dr. Albert Barnett (Atlantic Information Services, Inc.: Washington, D. C., 1997). He was a vice president of development for Pacific Mutual Insurance Company and a principal with William Mercer, Inc., an international benefits consulting firm. He is currently a full-time management consultant with his own firm and also serves as educational director of the Institute for Health Care Advancement.

Both Gloria and Tom are widely sought after speakers at national conferences. Together, they have written and published *The Health Insurance Alternative* (Putnam/Perigee: New York, New York, 1984), a consumer's guide to using HMOs.